Before Big School

Before Big School

A PRACTICAL PARENT'S GUIDE TO SCHOOL READINESS

WRITTEN BY DANIELLE MURRAY
ILLUSTRATED BY KATHERINE RICHARDSON

My child's name is

They start school in

First published in 2022 by Ethel Street Press

© Danielle Murray 2022

All rights reserved. Except as permitted under the Australian Copyright Act 1968 (for example, a fair dealing for the purposes of study, research, criticism or review), no part of this book may be reproduced, stored in a retrieval system, communicated or transmitted in any form or by any means without prior written permission.

ISBN: 978-0-646-85483-0

Illustrations, book and cover design by Katherine Richardson

Edited by Katherine Richardson

Disclaimer

The material in this publication is of the nature of general comment only, and does not represent professional advice. It is not intended to provide specific guidance for particular circumstances and it should not be relied on as the basis for any decision to take action or not take action on any matter which it covers. Readers should obtain professional advice where appropriate, before making any such decision. To the maximum extent permitted by law, the author and publisher disclaim all responsibility and liability to any person, arising directly or indirectly from any person taking or not taking action based on the information in this publication.

www.beforebigschool.com.au

For Kade, my beautiful baby boy.
Thank you for being you.

Contents

Foreword	11
Introduction	13
Chapter One: Early Literacy Skills	17
Chapter Two: Early Numeracy Skills	59
Chapter Three: Problem Solving Skills	85
Chapter Four: Nurturing Curiosity	91
Chapter Five: The Magic of Play	97
Chapter Six: Gross Motor Skills	107
Chapter Seven: Catering to Different Learning Styles	113
Chapter Eight: Managing Nerves	119
Chapter Nine: Independence and Organisation Skills	127
Chapter Ten: Social Skills and Friendships	137
Chapter Eleven: Resilience	143
Chapter Twelve: School Ready Checklist	153
Chapter Thirteen: Week One and Beyond	163

Foreword

This year my role changed from teacher to mother. I welcomed my little boy Kade into the world on the 25th of May, 2021. Motherhood, I am learning, shares many similarities with teaching. If I had to describe both roles, the chosen adjectives would be the same - challenging, rewarding, tiring. Patience is key, routine is vital, as is flexibility, and an enormous grin on a tiny face can make the hardest day worth it.

As parents, we want only the best for our children. We want to equip them with the tools they need to become confident, independent, resilient, and achieve success. One day, while Kade was napping, I began to think about when the time comes for him to start school. How would I ensure he was school ready? What skills would I want him to have before he stepped through the classroom door on his first day of Prep? How would I ensure he was ready emotionally, socially and academically? From these questions the idea for this book was born.

My aim with Before Big School is to share my knowledge and experience from the early childhood classroom to create a practical and informative guide for you – a parent looking to achieve school readiness for their child! The activities and strategies you'll find in this book have been tried, tested and tweaked time and time again with my Prep and Year One students. The knowledge I share has been collected from years of working with students in the early years and surrounding myself with exceptional teachers who aspire to reach every learner and cater to every learning style.

I hope this book proves to be a useful tool in helping you and your child achieve school readiness. As they step into that classroom on day one, my goal is that you both feel set up for success as they make the transition to big school.

Danielle

Introduction

Before we get into the how, let's start with the what.

What exactly does school readiness mean? A child who is school ready will possess the knowledge and skills needed to make a smooth transition into school.

School readiness involves the development of:

- Skills for learning.
- Effective communication skills.
- Social skills and emotional regulation.
- Organisational skills and independence.
- Fine and gross motor skills.

School readiness does not involve:

- Teaching your child to read and write.
- Teaching your child to complete basic maths problems.
- Replicating a school day or facilitating formal lessons at home.

School readiness is about equipping your child with the tools they need to succeed and to experience a positive start to school. Throughout this book we will explore the what and the how of each component of school readiness.

A few things to note:

- I am a teacher in Queensland where the first year of primary school is referred to as Prep. This is the same in Tasmania and Victoria. Prep is the equivalent to Kindergarten in New South Wales, Reception in South Australia and Transition in the Northern Territory.

- Some activities outlined in this book suggest the use of small objects such as beads or counters. These objects can be choking hazards so please remember to always supervise your child when they are working with these items. Always select items according to the age recommendations outlined by the manufacturer.

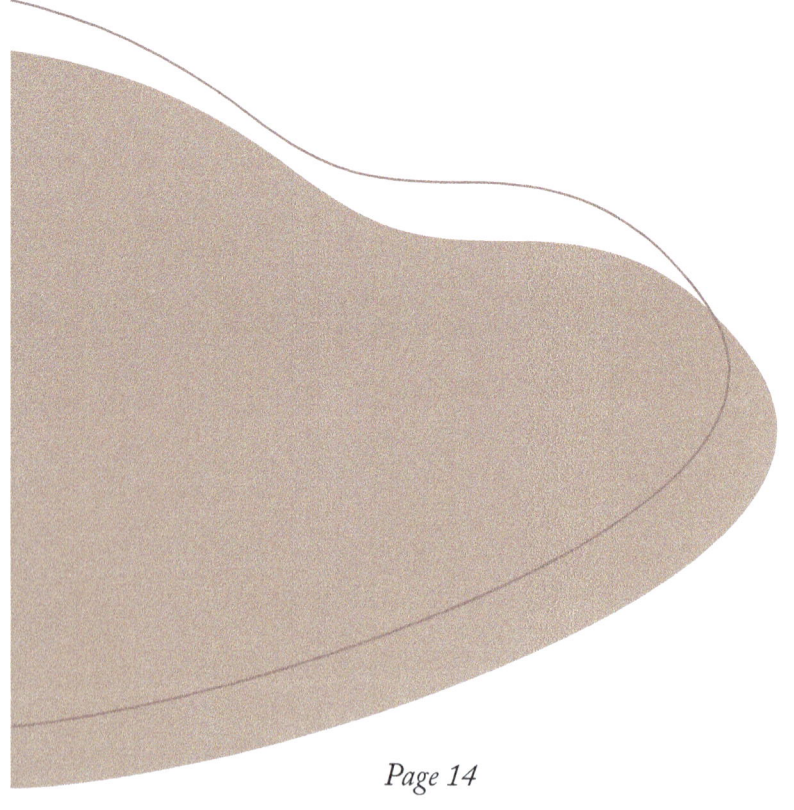

Early literacy should be incidental, play-based and most importantly - fun.

Chapter One

Early Literacy Skills

Literacy.

One small word, one huge concept, and one that I am extremely passionate about. Literacy is commonly defined as the ability to read, write, speak and listen. These skills are necessary, not only for your child to access the school curriculum, but to access basic tasks in their everyday life. Think about your day so far. How many times have you required literacy skills today? Reading and replying to text messages, conversing with co-workers, reading package labels, deciphering bus timetables, filling in forms - the list goes on. Literacy skills are an integral part of our daily lives and by supporting your child to develop early literacy skills, you are setting them up for the best chance of academic success, before they set foot in the classroom.

So, now we've covered the why, let's move onto the how. Early literacy skills are best developed through real world experiences, so look for those opportunities for teachable moments. Parents are their children's first teachers, and they play an important role in fostering an early love of learning. Leave the worksheets and structured learning activities for your child's teacher, they'll have many, many years of formal learning ahead of them.

Early literacy should be incidental, play-based and most importantly - fun.

Learning should cater to your child's interests and should never be forced. No flashcards, no worksheets, no textbooks. While these may seem like a simple path to school readiness, they don't always deliver the desired result. We don't want a battle on our hands before school even begins; we want to make learning magical. Your child isn't going to look back fondly on the times you revised using flashcards, but they will remember the time you hunted for dinosaur eggs at the park, or spent a rainy afternoon turning the living room into a cinema. These magical play experiences provide perfect opportunities for teachable moments.

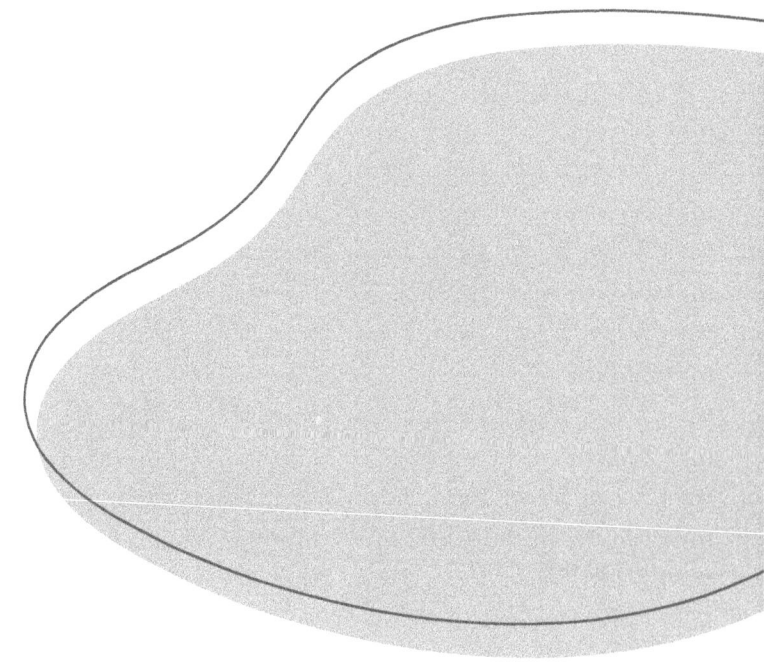

Reading

Early literacy is not about teaching your child how to read. What we want to do is spark a life-long love of books and nurture an *interest* in reading. We want to equip our children with the early literacy skills they will later need to become successful readers.

There may be one downside to raising an avid reader – you'll likely find yourself being hounded to read *just one more story* to your bookworm at bedtime each night.

Parents of my students often come to me with a common concern - *my child just doesn't like to read*. These parents are often facing battles at home when it comes time to complete their home readers. The task of completing home readers can often be met with reluctance from children (and their parents). So, what is the solution when a child shows no interest in books? Finding that one book. That one perfect book that reels your child in and transforms them into a reader. A reluctant reader of mine discovered the *Pig the Pug* books after her family welcomed a bug-eyed pooch into their home - that was the book that turned her into a reader. She devoured the entire collection of books before embarking on a trip to the bookstore in search of her next read. Her mother was thrilled, yet asked me if it was a problem that her daughter still wasn't completing her assigned home readers. My answer was no, she was reading!

As a teacher, I've seen the benefits of reading firsthand. Children who love books and are consistently read to tend to have larger vocabularies. Books expose children to words they would not necessarily encounter in daily life. Books help them to develop vivid imaginations, stronger speaking and listening skills, and struggle less with the writing process. A confident reader, in time, will become a confident writer. Children who read often have a greater understanding of emotions and are able to empathise with others, as they are frequently exposed to the feelings of others through characters in stories.

It's never too early (or too late) to start reading to your child. I started reading to my son the very first week we brought him home from the hospital. While reading to a newborn baby felt a little silly at first, there is a lot of research supporting the importance of reading for literacy development from birth. Aim to make reading part of your daily routine with your child. If you have a spare few minutes before you head out the door in the morning, grab a book. Prioritise reading and think of it like brushing your teeth each day, something you do no matter what.

Tips and Tricks for Reading with Your Child

Before You Read

Learning begins before we even open a book. While it might be tempting to flip open the cover and dive straight into the story, first pause and take a look at the front cover. Guide your child to take a close look at the pictures. Have a conversation and ask questions. For example, "What do you think is going to happen in the story?" and, "Why?" Asking these open-ended questions encourages your child to think deeply, express opinions and make text-to-self connections.

Predicting is an important skill for learning and children make predictions using their knowledge and past experiences. For example, they might see a picture of a character wearing goggles and floaties and use these clues to make a prediction. They might say, "I think the little boy is going to go swimming because he is wearing goggles and floaties. When I go to swimming lessons, I wear floaties and goggles in the pool."

Modelling is a powerful tool so share your own ideas and thinking with your child. For example, if there was a picture of a boy holding a suitcase and smiling you might say, "I think the little boy in the story is going on a holiday. This is because I can see he's holding a suitcase. I think he's happy to be going on holidays because I can see a big smile on his face." Allow time for your child to make connections to their own life and share stories and ideas.

Read the title of the book, explain that a title gives us clues about what will happen in the story. Introduce the author and illustrator. Explain that an author's job is to write the story and an illustrator's job is to draw the pictures.

As You Read

When reading a story to your child, think of it as an opportunity to model what good readers do. Good readers read with expression (not like a robot), they don't read too fast or too slow and they stop at full stops. Children need to listen frequently to good reading in order to become good readers themselves. Have fun with the story. Give the character's unique voices, change your voice to suit the emotions being experienced by the character and sound enthusiastic about what you're reading. If the character is a giant, give them a big booming voice. If the character is nervous give them a quiet voice that shakes. Bring the characters and story to life.

As you read, give your child time to take in the pictures. Help them to understand that pictures are an important part of the story, they give us extra information and help us to understand the story. Point out the character's facial expressions, "He is feeling sad - I know this because he has a frown, his head is down, and I can see he is crying." This helps your child to understand emotions.

When you read, show your child the correct way to open a book. Show them where to start reading from by pointing to the first word on the page and explain that we read from left to right. Demonstrate how to turn the pages of a book carefully without tearing or folding them. Point to the words on the page as you read them to help them make links between the written words and the words they are hearing.

After You Read

Once you've finished reading, talk to your child about the story. Avoid closed questions like, "Did you like the book?" and instead, ask them to share what they liked about the story, their favourite part, which characters they like or dislike. Share your own opinions and model giving reasons. For example, "I liked it when the witch made a new broom because it had something that all the characters liked."

Talk about the events in the story. Support your child to retell the events in the story in order (beginning, middle, end). You can begin to introduce the basic structure of a story by explaining how each part of a story has a job. The beginning of the story introduces the characters and where the story is taking place. In the middle of the story there is a challenge or problem which the character must overcome, and the end is where the character solves the problem.

Support your child to make text-to-self connections. If

the character went on holiday, allow time for your child to talk about the last holiday your family went on. If the character in the story felt excited about something, talk to your child about a time when they were excited. This will help your child to develop empathy and emotional intelligence as they begin to understand and relate to the emotions of others.

Encourage Self Selection of Books

Visit a bookshop or library and support your child to select their own books. Be guided by their interests. If the current obsession is dinosaurs go with it; hunt for fiction and non-fiction books about dinosaurs. You can help your child to select a book which is right for them by ensuring it is age appropriate.

Read the Story More Than Once

Does your child have a favourite book that you find yourself reading over and over again? While reading this book three times a night for the past month can feel tedious, there are actually some amazing benefits for your little one. You've likely memorised every word in the story and guess what? So have they. They may be able to recite the story, beginning to end, along with you. This does wonders for building their confidence as they experience success and begin to see themselves as a reader. Repetitive reading also helps your child develop reading fluency. As they recite the story, they'll mimic that great reading you've been modelling for them.

Reading in the Real World

Reading should not just be limited to bedtime stories. Children need to be exposed to a wide variety of text types. They need to understand that text appears everywhere in their environment and that reading is an important life skill. Read to your child while cooking; by reading them a recipe you're exposing them to a new text type (a procedural text) and helping them to understand that different texts have different purposes. Read packages in the supermarket, signs in the street and birthday invitations from friends. Point out letters and talk about the sounds they make. Writing is everywhere which makes finding opportunities for teachable moments a breeze.

Booklist

For children in the early years, I love books that are fun to read. Look for books with rhyming words, repetition, characters who are silly, funny or kind, and characters who push boundaries and challenge stereotypes.

Here are just a few of my favourite books to read with children:

- *The Gruffalo* by Julia Donaldson
- *Room on the Broom* by Julia Donaldson (Quite possibly my favourite children's book of all time.)
- *Possum Magic* by Mem Fox
- *Ten Little Fingers and Ten Little* Toes by Mem Fox
- *Koala Lou* by Mem Fox
- *Pig the Pug* by Aaron Blabey
- *Pearl Barley and Charlie Parsley* by Aaron Blabey
- *Wombat Stew* by Marcia Vaughan
- *Giraffes Can't Dance* by Giles Andreae
- *Rose Meets Mr Wintergarten* by Bob Graham
- *Mr McGee* by Pamela Allen
- *Grandpa and Thomas* by Pamela Allen
- *The Very Cranky Bear* by Nick Bland
- *The Very Super Bear* by Nick Bland

- *Our Skin: A First Conversation About Race* by Megan Madison and Jessica Ralli
- *Magic Beach* by Alison Lester
- *The Pout Pout Fish* by Deborah Diesen
- *The Rainbow Fish* by Marcus Pfister
- *Our Class is a Family* by Shannon Olsen
- *The Day the Crayons Quit* by Drew Daywait
- *We're Going on a Bear Hunt* by Michael Rosen

Phonological Awareness

Phonological awareness is the ability to hear and manipulate sounds. Phonological awareness skills are important pre-reading skills and are linked to strong reading abilities. Building these skills will help to prepare your child for the big job of learning to read.

Phonological awareness skills include rhyming (words with similar endings), alliteration (words beginning with the same sound), identifying syllables (word parts), sentence and word segmentation (breaking up the word or sentence into parts), onset and rime (beginning and ending sounds in words) and recognising phonemes (individual sounds).

To build phonological awareness, encourage your child to play and experiment with words and sounds.

Activities to Develop Phonological Awareness Skills

Rhyme

For children to master rhyme, they must first hear and recognise it before finally being able to produce it. This means children need lots of opportunities to listen to and talk about rhyming words before we can expect them to be able to create rhyme themselves.

Read Books That Rhyme

Rhyming books are lots of fun to read with your child. Julia Donaldson's books (*Room on the Broom*, *The Gruffalo* and *The Gruffalo's Child*) are some of my favourite rhyming books to read with children. As you read, draw your child's attention to the rhyming words on each page. Explain that rhyming words are words that have the same ending sound. You could say, "I think I can hear some rhyming words on this page. Remember, rhyming words have the same ending sound. Listen to these two words - should and wood. They rhyme because they both have the *ood* sound at the end. Can you say those two words - should and wood?"

Recite Nursery Rhymes Together

Nursery rhymes are packed full of rhyming couplets (pairs of rhyming words) and are perfect as an early introduction to rhyming words. They're usually silly or funny, as well as short in length, two things which make them easy for your child to remember and recite.

Do They Rhyme?

Once your child has had lots of opportunities to hear rhyme, you can start to work on their ability to recognise rhyme. A really simple way to do this is to say two words and ask your child to show you a thumbs up if they think the words rhyme or a thumbs down if they don't. Start with simple words like *cat and bat* or *cot and dot*.

Odd One Out

Challenge your child to pick out the word that doesn't rhyme from a list of words. For example, "I'm going to say three words. Listen to them carefully and tell me which word doesn't rhyme - *sock, lock, bat.*"

Matching Games

You can easily create a matching game by printing off rhyming pictures (there are plenty already made online) and sticking them onto Lego pieces or other building blocks. Ask your child to find the matching pairs. You could write rhyming words onto Lego pieces and support your child by reading the words out loud as they find the rhyming pairs. Games like rhyming bingo are also fun and helpful.

Producing Rhyme

Once your child is confident in recognising rhyming words, invite them to have a go at producing rhyme independently. Model the skill first. You could say, "I'm thinking of words that rhyme with *top*, I can think of *mop*, *shop* and *bop*." Start off simple, ask them to think of a word that rhymes with a short word like *cat*. If your child comes up with nonsense words, this is completely fine. As long as the words they produce have the same ending sound, you can be sure they understand the concept. If they're struggling to think of rhyming words, this means they need more time to hear rhyme and consolidate their understanding, so go back and spend some more time sharing nursery rhymes and rhyming stories together.

Syllables

The ability to break words into syllables will benefit children greatly when they read and write. Decoding is a skill used in reading to sound out unknown words. It involves breaking the word apart and using letter and sound knowledge. Knowledge of syllables helps greatly with decoding. When we break words apart to spell them, for example *sub-stan-tial*, we are applying our knowledge of syllables.

Use Actions and Movement

Practise breaking words and names apart into syllables - *ma gic (2), mon-key (2), um-brell-a (3)*. Clap, jump or stomp on each syllable. Clap your child's name and count the syllables - *Cal-vin (2)*.

Supermarket Syllables

Next time you're shopping, choose objects to break into syllables as you put them into the trolley.

For example, *ba-na-na (3)* or *bis-cuit (2)*.

Word and Sentence Segmentation

When children segment sentences into their word parts, they learn to hear individual words within a sentence. When they segment words, they learn to hear individual sounds and word parts.

Break it Up

Practise breaking apart compound words. For example, "Say the word *firefly*, take away *fly*, what is left?"

Practise saying a sentence and counting the words using your fingers. For example, "How many words do you hear in this sentence? *I went to the park.*" Have your child jump, clap, hop, click or stomp to represent each word in a sentence. You can also use blocks, Lego, post-it notes or counters to represent the words in a sentence. Say a sentence like, "I went to the beach," and ask them to place an object in front of them for each word they hear.

Onset and Rime

Onset refers to the beginning sound in a word. Rime refers to the group of letters that follow. For example, *c-at*, c is the onset, *at* is the rime. By teaching children onset and rime we teach them about beginning sounds and word families which will assist them with spelling in the future.

Hand Actions

Have your child hold out one hand for the onset, one hand for the rime and clap their hands together as they say the whole word. Ensure the onset is the left hand and rime is the right hand to encourage understanding of correct text direction when reading and writing.

Recognising Phonemes

Recognising phonemes (sounds) helps children to understand how sounds are put together to build words. They must be able to recognise phonemes before they are able to read and write.

Beginning Sounds

Point out objects in your child's environment and talk about the sound they start with. For example, "That's a tree - it starts with the *t* sound. Tractor, tricycle, and toys also start with the *t* sound."

Look out for objects that begin with the same letter as your child's name, like *Sam* and *sign*. Talk about how they have the same beginning letter and sound.

When reading, point out individual letters and talk about the sounds they make. Invite your child to think of other words that start with the same sound.

If your child is confident at recognising beginning sounds, ask them to have a go at identifying final sounds. For example, "What is the last sound you can hear in the word *dog*?"

I Spy

Look at pictures in a book and play *I spy*. For example, "I spy with my little eye, something beginning with *t*." Give your child time to examine the page and find the object on the page that begins with the letter *t*.

CVC (Consonant Vowel Consonant) Words

If your child is confident with beginning and end sounds, introduce them to CVC words. These are three letter words that begin and end with a consonant and have a short vowel in the middle.

For example, *c-a-t* and *d-o-g*. Ask your child if they can identify all the sounds in a CVC word.

Alliteration

Alliteration is a fun way to build knowledge of beginning sounds. Sentences using alliteration are fun to say and often sound silly which is why children enjoy them.

Silly Sentences

Create silly sentences with your child. For example, *Magic monkeys munch mangoes* or use your child's name, *Silly Sam sails sailboats steadily.*

Tongue Twisters

Recite tongue twisters with your child. For example, *Peter Piper picked a peck of pickled peppers.*

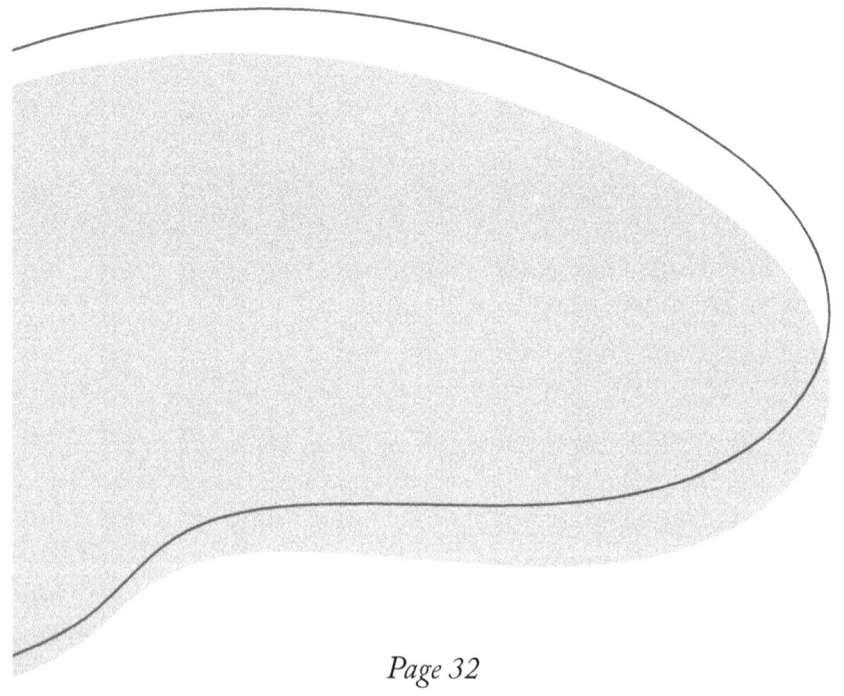

Letter and Sound Knowledge

Letter and sound knowledge is an important piece of the reading puzzle. A child who has letter and sound knowledge will understand that letters are symbols that represent sounds and that these letters can be put together to form words. They will be able to recite the alphabet song and recognise uppercase and lowercase letters and the sounds they make. Remember, it's not necessary for your child to know all twenty-six letters before beginning school. A great place to start is with the letters in their name. Focus on sound recognition of these letters first before moving onto the rest of the alphabet.

Activities to Develop Letter and Sound Knowledge

Songs

There are a number of excellent phonics songs on YouTube that are helpful in developing letter and sound knowledge. Jolly Phonics is a fantastic resource - I like to begin our morning in Prep each day with the Jolly Phonics song to consolidate letter and sound knowledge. It combines sounds and hand actions with a catchy tune that makes it easy to remember. The YouTube clip also displays each letter which helps in connecting the written letter with the sound it makes.

Sing the alphabet song with your child. Aim for them to be able to confidently recite the song independently and in the correct order.

Sorting

Magnetic letters are a fantastic tool for sorting letters. Set up plastic bowls in different colours and have your child sort the magnetic letters. You could try asking them to hunt for one letter at a time, for example, "Let's look for all the letter *a* magnets and put them in the red bowl." Burying the magnets in sand and having your child dig for letters before sorting is a great way to make this activity really hands-on.

Use pictures from catalogues or magazines to create a matching activity. Cut out pictures from a grocery or toy catalogue and challenge your child to match the objects with their beginning letter. You could write the alphabet with chalk on concrete outside or lay out alphabet magnets on the floor or table and sort household objects according to their beginning letter and sound. You could also use small objects and cups labelled with letters. If your child enjoys collage you could have them paste the pictures under their matching letters on paper.

Games

- Write letters in large writing on concrete using chalk. Say a letter sound or letter name and ask your child to jump on to the matching letter. Begin with just a few letters at a time.

- Write letters on cards and place them in a bag. Invite your child to pull out a lucky dip and name the letter and the sound it makes. Bonus points if they can also tell you a word that starts with the corresponding sound.

- Create a letter hunt in your house or backyard by hiding letter cards. Give your child a list of letters to hunt for and have them tick each one off as they find it. When reading, hunt for letters on the pages of the book. You can make this explicit by focussing on hunting for one letter at a time, or leaving it open by asking, "How many letters on this page do you know?"

Pre-Writing Skills

Before children are able to write, they must develop pre-writing skills. These skills are the building blocks for tracing, copying, drawing, writing and colouring. An essential pre-writing skill involves practising the shapes and strokes that letters and numbers consist of. Pre-writing skills also involve fine motor development to strengthen little fingers and hands.

Your child may already be beginning to experiment with writing. They may mimic you by pretending to write and make scribbles on paper. Once your child has started to show an interest in wanting to write there are a number of ways you can support their development of pre-writing skills.

Fine Motor Skill Development

Fine motor skill development is essential for writing and pencil grip, as well as tasks in everyday life. We want to strengthen the muscles in the hands and fingers and develop coordination, so our children are able to manipulate small objects such as pencils and scissors. These skills are important for a number of tasks in the classroom like writing, drawing, painting, cutting, or using a glue stick.

Activities to Support Fine Motor Development

Using Scissors

Give your child frequent opportunities to safely use scissors. Start by letting them practise cutting through playdough before moving on to cutting strips of paper. You can then print out shapes on a page for use on collage or art and craft activities and encourage them to cut them out. Provide a range of different mediums for cutting practise like cardboard, alfoil and different types of paper.

Ensure your child is using a correct grip when using scissors:

1. Thumb is placed on top through the small hole.

2. Other three fingers are placed through the larger hole.

3. Item being cut is held in the opposite hand.

Threading

Use beads and string or elastic to make jewellery or other items.

Colouring In

Challenge your child to colour carefully in the lines.

Playdough Manipulation

Create objects using playdough.

Chopsticks

Provide kids chopsticks and pompoms. Invite your child to move the pompoms from one place to another using the chopsticks.

Art

Allow time for your child to draw and paint.

Everyday Items

Have your child practise everyday tasks like opening packets or buttoning shirts and pants. Using pegs to hang out washing (or just playing with pegs) is also fantastic for fine motor development.

Lego or Duplo

Connecting and removing blocks is great for building up those finger muscles and developing coordination.

Tweezers

Grab an ice-cube tray, tweezers and mini pom poms and have your child transfer the pom poms into the ice-cube tray using the tweezers.

Gardening

Get out in the garden and have your child dig, pull weeds and plant seeds and seedlings.

Rubber Bands

Thread rubber bands or elastics onto an object such as a paddlepop stick or paper towel roll.

Button Pictures

Draw patterns such as zigzags or swirly lines on card and have your child place buttons onto the lines.

Sticky Dot Art

Newsagents sell pages of dot stickers. These can be used for art and craft activities. Children love peeling stickers and this is great for fine motor development.

Pencil Grip

An incorrect pencil grip can be difficult to correct. When beginning Prep, some children arrive with an established pencil grip, often one that isn't quite right. Your child likely grasps pencils and crayons with their whole first, but you can support them to learn the correct pencil grip. This will take time, lots of practise and lots of modelling from you and their teacher to master. A correct pencil grip requires the *Pincer Grasp*. This is the ability to pick up small objects using the thumb and index finger. Lots of engagement in fine motor skill activities will be helpful in further developing this skill.

Ensure your child is using a correct pencil grip:

1. Hold the pencil between the thumb and pointer finger.
2. Tuck the other three fingers in towards the palm.
3. Rest the pencil against the end of the middle finger.

When teaching pencil grip, I ask the children to imagine the pencil is a car. Mum and Dad are in the front (thumb and pointer finger) and the three kids are in the back (middle, ring, and pinkie fingers). You can also get rubber pencil grips that have divots for fingers to rest in, these are really helpful for practising the correct grip.

Pattern Writing

Pattern writing is practising the lines and shapes needed to correctly form letters and numbers. Once your child is confident at producing simple marks such as scribbles, dots, and circles, pattern writing activities can be introduced before they begin attempting formal writing.

Shapes and lines to practise:

- Circles and dots (practise drawing big or small and creating circles in different directions)
- Straight lines (assists with letters E, F, H, I, L and T)
- Zigzag lines (assists with letters A, M, V, W and Z)
- Curved lines (assists with letters C, O, Q, U)
- Crosses (assists with letter X)
- Spiral lines (assists with spatial awareness)

Support your child to practise pattern writing in different mediums - not just pencil and paper. You can use chalk, scented pens, paint, crayon, felt pen or even glitter glue. Setting up trays of shaving cream or slime is a fun way to practise pattern writing. Create a picture of a landscape or a treasure map with an X to mark the spot. Dot to dot colouring books are also a great way for your child to practise straight lines. You'll find tons of pattern writing worksheets online, these are great if your child is enthusiastic, but remember, don't force it. Early learning should be fun.

Drawing Pictures

Drawing pictures is an important pre-writing skill. Children progress from scribbling to drawing simple, recognisable pictures. Children use drawing as a means of communication and to express themselves: before they can write, they use pictures to tell stories. If your child enjoys drawing, you could ask them to draw a picture to demonstrate their understanding after reading a story.

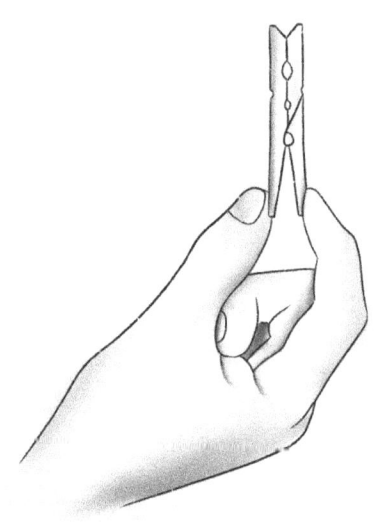

Writing

Once your child has demonstrated pattern writing abilities, they can begin to experiment with letter formation. There is no need to push your child into learning letter formation for the whole alphabet before they're ready. There is a huge focus in Prep on teaching the correct formation of uppercase and lowercase letters. Sometimes, despite their good intentions, parents can teach their children to form letters incorrectly. Handwriting has changed since most parents were in primary school. Also, as children progress from primary to high school there is less of a push to practise correct handwriting, as most work is completed digitally. When adults write, it is usually done quickly with little thought as to how the letters are formed. These factors can all lead to the development of incorrect habits in letter formation, and these can be tricky to reverse.

If you feel that your child is ready, meaning they've mastered pattern writing, can hold a pencil correctly and have expressed an interest in writing letters, you can start practising with them at home. To ensure you're teaching the correct letter formation for the state or territory you live in, obtain a letter formation chart which shows the correct way to write each letter. These charts are available digitally or in physical paper form and will feature arrows and numbers which show the direction and order of steps for each letter. Approach letter formation as you would pattern writing - make it fun and hands-on.

When formal handwriting is taught, the letters of the alphabet are taught in a particular order, grouped by similarities in formation. The uppercase letters are taught first. In Prep however, letter formation is often taught in order of whichever phonics approach is used by the school.

The order of letters for handwriting is:
- Straight letters (letter i, t, l, x, z)
- Clockwise letters (m, n, h, r, b, p, j)
- Anti-clockwise letters (c, d, q, f, o, e)
- Double rotation letters (g, y, s)

Activities for Letter Formation

Print A4 size letters (begin with uppercase) on paper and laminate if possible. These will come in handy for a range of letter formation activities.

Sensory Table

Create a sensory table to practise letter formation. Trays of coloured rice, sand, shaving cream and slime provide fun opportunities to practise writing letters. Sometimes using a finger, rather than a pencil, can make children more inclined to give it a go. If they make a mistake, it can simply be wiped away, ready for another attempt.

Playdough

Make or buy a batch of playdough and have your child use this to form the letters of the alphabet. Playdough can be placed over the top of laminated letters.

Mix it Up

Provide different mediums for letter writing, such as chalk, paint, felt pens, glitter glue, crayons, coloured pencils and whiteboard markers. Encourage your child to have a go at writing the letters of the alphabet using one of these tools. Model the correct formation first and then invite them to try. Fun stationary can be a great incentive; reluctant editors in my Year Three class really benefited from being allowed to use scented gel pens to make their corrections.

Toy Cars

Toy cars can be used to trace letters. Place the toy car on the starting point and use the shape of the letter as a road for the car to drive along.

Name Writing

There's one exception to my rule of waiting until your child is ready to introduce letter formation and that is when it comes to writing their own name. I strongly believe that all children should be able to, or be getting closer to being able to, recognise and write their first name correctly before beginning school. Children at school must recognise and write their name frequently. They must recognise their name when they look for their bag on the rack outside the classroom or when their hat gets mixed up with others. They will also be frequently required to write their name on worksheets and belongings.

Children must be able to recognise their own name before they can even begin thinking about writing it. Spend time showing your child their name. Write it for them, point it out when you see it written somewhere and include it in their environment. Label their belongings with their name and display it in their room. They need to see their name frequently before they will be able to recognise it.

Once they are able to recognise their name, begin teaching them how to write it. Write their name in large letters and have them trace over it using paint or glitter glue. Provide lots of practise using those different mediums we talked about earlier, and also provide opportunities to practise with pencil and paper. Write your child's name for them and have them copy it. They will need lots of practise before they will be able to remember how to write it independently. Ensure you remind your child to begin their name with an uppercase letter, followed by lowercase letters. This is easy to forget and can become a habit which will require correcting. By explaining that all names begin with an uppercase letter we begin to develop an understanding of punctuation, which can later become one of the trickiest components of writing.

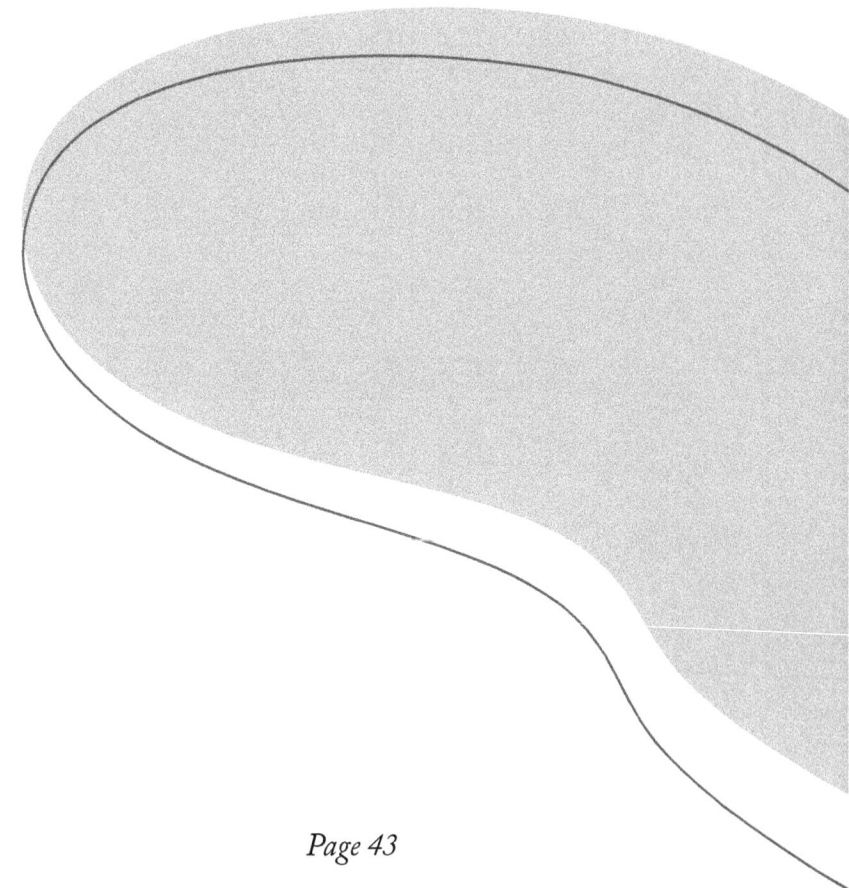

Speaking and Listening

I believe that one of the most important steps you can take to ensure your child is ready for school is to develop their communication skills. These skills allow children to access the curriculum effectively and communicate well with their peers and teachers. Speaking and listening skills are used numerous times over the course of a school day and in all aspects of learning. They're needed to comprehend information, to follow instructions, to participate in class discussion, to interact and collaborate with peers and to socialise at break times.

Before children become successful readers and writers, they must become confident speakers and listeners. As parents, it's our job to provide with them with plenty of opportunities to practise their speaking and listening skills in daily life. In a world filled with electronic devices, the art of conversation is at risk of being lost.

Activities to Develop Speaking Skills

Talk to Your Child

Sounds obvious right? Unfortunately, life gets busy, and it can be hard to fit time into your day for quality conversations. With the frantic rush of childcare and school pickups and drop-offs, grocery shopping, appointments, meal preparation, bedtime routines and a whole lot more, it can be hard to find the time to foster rich conversations.

Children learn to speak from those around them. As a parent, remember, you are your child's first teacher. Modelling effective communication is the most powerful tool in your toolbox for teaching your child effective speaking skills. Practise makes perfect so we need to provide quality speaking opportunities frequently throughout our day. When speaking to your child, model speaking the way you would like them to speak. Use eye contact, speak politely, ask questions, listen actively, and give them your full attention. Often adults become frustrated when children appear distracted while they are speaking to them, so we need to put down the phone and listen if we expect this from them.

In the car after Kindergarten or childcare, share something about your day. It could be something interesting or funny that happened, or even something you found challenging. Talk about how it made you feel and invite your child to share something about their day. We want to avoid closed questions like, "How was your day?" as these invite closed answers such as, "Good," or, "Okay." Instead, try asking, "Can you tell me something you did today that was fun?"

When your child is playing independently, engage them in conversation about their play. Ask open questions that require your child to explain what they're doing or making. Children have the most amazing imaginations and it's fascinating to hear their thought processes as they play. When your child builds or draws or creates a masterpiece made from cardboard boxes, ask them to explain their process.

The grocery store provides countless opportunities for conversation and chances to introduce new words. You can point out different items and talk to your child about them. For example, "This is a lychee, on the outside it is pink and bumpy but inside it is smooth and white. It tastes very sweet." Share opinions and listen to theirs, "My favourite fruit is mango because it is sweet and juicy.

Which fruit is your favourite? Can you tell me why you like it?"

Being mindful of providing opportunities for quality conversations with your child will allow you to look out for opportunities in your day. It can be as simple as introducing a new word as you're driving in the car. For example, "That sign over there says pedestrian crossing. Can you say those words? Do you know what they mean?" Broaden their knowledge of words and spark their curiosity.

Allow time for your child to talk about their interests. When children are passionate about something, the words flow. Ask lots of questions and expand their knowledge if it's a topic you know about. If it's not, take some time to find out about it together.

Speaking to Adults

Speaking to adults can be quite daunting for children, especially if they haven't had much practise. A school day can require children to speak to adults for a variety of reasons. Greeting their teacher and responding to questions, asking for help or to use the bathroom (this is an important one), ordering from the tuckshop and greeting office ladies are just a few examples. These scenarios may not seem like a big deal to us, but to a young child they can feel huge.

We model these skills for our children every day, your child's mind is like a sponge. When you greet the lady scanning the groceries, thank the waiter in a café or say good morning to the man you're passing on the path, your child soaks this up. In addition to modelling these skills, we need to provide real life opportunities for children to put them into practise. Start small, encourage your child to thank the waiter when they're served food at a café or restaurant or greet a familiar adult using their name. Build up to bigger things like thanking a relative for having them over at their house or ordering their own food at a café or restaurant. You can make these tasks feel a little less daunting by role playing them at home. Remember to notice and praise, "I love how you said thank you to Jane's mum when she gave you cake." We want to reinforce and celebrate great speaking skills.

When familiar adults, such as relatives or friends come over, encourage your child to greet them using their name and initiate a conversation by asking a question. The question can be as simple as asking them, "How are you?" This skill will take time, lots of practise and maybe some gentle reminders.

Turn Taking

Taking turns is an important conversation skill and one that little people often struggle with. They just love to interrupt and it's usually because they're busting to tell you what's on their mind. Calling out is a tough one to combat in the classroom. It takes lots of practise, patience and persistence, as will teaching your child to turn take when engaging in conversation. You can practise this at home with your child by taking turns to ask and respond to questions. Your little one might need some gentle reminders at first to remember to wait their turn. Avoid answering questions for your child and allow them time to process the question and respond. Too often we rush in and answer for them, meanwhile the cogs were still turning in their head as they processed what was being asked and formulated a response.

When practising turn taking, we help to reinforce active listening and discourage talking over the top of others. You could even introduce a prop, like a wand or stuffed toy, to reinforce this skill. For example, "When I'm holding the magic wand, it's my turn to ask a question. When I give it to you it's your turn to answer."

Open Ended Questions

Earlier we spoke about the importance of open-ended questions in banishing answers such as *yes*, *no* and *good*. We want to ask questions that encourage children to explain and describe, or to share ideas and opinions. For example, you might see your child constructing an elaborate object out of boxes and ask:

- "What are you making?"
- "How did you make it? What was the first step?"
- "Why did you decide to make that?"
- "Which part was the trickiest?"

Often, during parent teacher interviews, parents will express their frustration when asking the question, "What did you do at school today?" and hearing, "Nothing." Upon attending the parent teacher interview, their child's very full workbooks sprawled in front of them, they would emit a subtle sigh of relief as they discovered that their child did not in fact do *nothing* at school each day. The school day is jam packed, it's super busy and questions like that can be overwhelming. After a busy day of learning, it's often easier to just say nothing. Help your child out by making your questions more specific.

You could ask:

- "What did you play at lunchtime and who did you play with?"
- "What did you learn in Maths today?"

- "What was the best part of your day?"
- "Did you do anything that was tricky today?"
- "What did you do in your sports lesson today?"

Your child is brimming with unique ideas and an astonishing imagination. When you throw out an open-ended question you never quite know what you'll get.

Try some of these just for fun:

- "What is something that you think you're really good at?"
- "If you could have a superpower, what would it be?"
- "Would you rather be able to fly or be invisible? Why?"

Speaking in Full Sentences (Importance for Writing)

A quote I once heard had a profound effect on my practise. It changed the way I taught writing in the early years. The quote reads, "You can't write it if you can't say it and you can't say it if you haven't heard it a lot!" – Pie Corbett. Teaching children to write in complete sentences is a challenge. They require plenty of opportunities to listen to sentences through reading and conversations with adults. When introducing sentence writing in the early years, we spend a lot of time constructing sentences orally. We turn and tell our buddy our sentence out loud before we have a go at writing it down.

Children who speak well, write well. Encouraging your child to speak in complete sentences will support their writing down the track. Often, children who struggle to grasp punctuation later in schooling don't speak in full sentences and therefore are unable to grasp sentence boundaries. They write run on sentences as they can't decide where to place full stops.

A strategy you can use to encourage full sentences is

to prompt your child to use the words from a question they're asked to answer it. For example, when your child is asked the question, "What is your favourite colour?" and their answer is "Blue," or, "Pink," prompt them to answer using the sentence starter, "My favourite colour is…" We can model this ourselves when we answer questions asked by our children.

Activities to Develop Listening Skills

Model Whole Body Listening

Whole body listening helps children to understand the behaviours needed to listen effectively. Before giving a set of verbal instructions, I check in with my class to ensure they are demonstrating the four components of whole body listening. I model and list each component and have my students repeat back what I'm saying and copy the behaviour. The four behaviours I look for are:

- Eyes are looking (we show the person who is speaking that we are listening by looking at them when they speak)
- Brain is thinking (we concentrate on understanding what the person is saying)
- Mouth is closed (we don't speak at the same time as someone else)
- Body is still (we keep our hands and feet still and don't fiddle when someone is speaking)

Reinforcing these behaviours can support children to avoid distractions and be more focused when listening to others. We can support them in being whole body listeners by modelling these four desired behaviours when we listen to our children speak, as well as prompting them to demonstrate the behaviours when they listen to others. Practising turn taking when conversing with your child is a great time to model and reinforce whole body listening.

Giving Verbal Instructions

When giving verbal instructions to children it can sometimes feel as if they haven't listened to a word you've said. In the classroom, as students move to their desks you cross your fingers and hope to not hear the dreaded whisper, "What are we doing again?"

Here are a few tried and tested tricks for giving verbal instructions:

- Start by capturing your child's attention and ensuring they are tuned in before you begin. This is a good time to reinforce the four components of whole body listening. You can do this by saying, "I need to tell you something and I need you to show me that you're listening. Can you show me whole body listening before I start?"
- Make your instructions short and simple.
- Ask your child to repeat back what you have asked them to do to ensure they have understood.

Being able to follow simple verbal instructions is a necessary skill for the classroom. Lots of practise before school begins will help get your child into the habit of tuning in and following instructions effectively.

Listening Games

Listening games allow children to practise their listening skills in an enjoyable way.

- Games like Simon Says are ideal. Throwing in multi-step instructions like, "Hop on one leg, then touch the ground," are a great way to challenge your child once they grasp the concept of the game. When played with a group it's also a great way to share the leadership role and reinforce turn taking.

- Musical Statues provides an opportunity for children to hone their listening skills and practise whole body listening. Ask them to freeze and make eye contact with you when the music stops. This one is also great for practising impulse control.
- I Spy (with a twist) can be used to practise listening skills and test out letter-sound knowledge. Start with a letter, "I spy with my little eye, something starting with *a*". "Well done! Apple is right. Before we move on to the next object, I want you to tell me something else that starts with the *a* sound, just like apple".
- Come up with your own listening games by assigning actions to specific words. For example, you could say, "When I say the word *banana* you're going to hop to the kitchen. When I say the word *cherry*, you're going to do a star jump. When I say the word *grape* you're going to jump up and down on the spot."

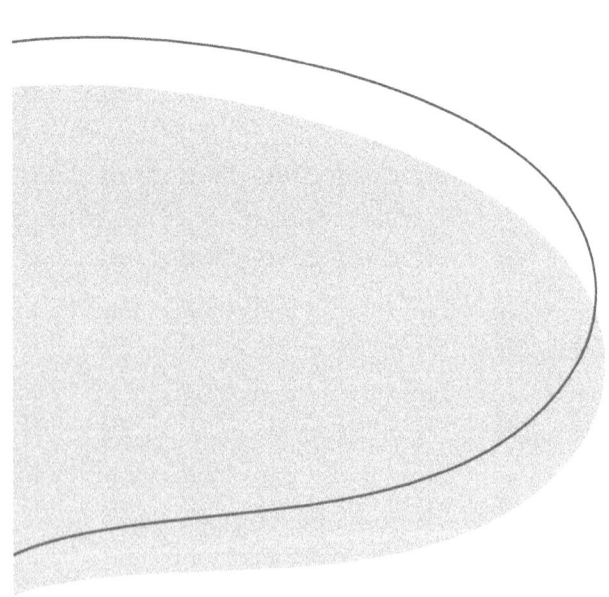

Building Vocabulary

In order for children to communicate effectively, they need to build their vocabulary. Understanding and being able to use a wide variety of words will allow your child to be more precise when expressing themselves. As children become more competent readers, and reach for more complex texts, they will encounter a range of words. Unfamiliar words will cause difficulties in comprehending the text. A large vocabulary will minimize comprehension issues and have a positive effect on overall reading and writing outcomes.

To build a child's vocabulary we need to expose them to an array of different words and model how to use them correctly. Children will need to hear a word more than once in order to grasp how to use it correctly. For example, you might introduce the word frightened when reading a book by saying, "This word is frightened, it means the same as scared. The little girl in the story was feeling scared or frightened. Do you remember a time when you felt frightened?" You might prompt your child to use the word by introducing a sentence starter, for example, "I felt frightened when…" On another occasion you might use the word in an everyday situation, for example, "I felt frightened when I heard that loud noise." Hearing a new word multiple times and used in a variety of ways will ensure they have a solid understanding of its meaning.

When speaking to children, don't be afraid to use big words, they'll often ask you what they mean. I once taught a little boy who had an insatiable curiosity for words. When we read a story in class his hand would shoot up, eager to find out what a word meant before I'd had a chance to ask if anyone knew what it meant. He'd often tell me new words he'd learnt, explaining what they meant and proudly using them in a sentence. This curiosity about words is what we need to encourage in our children. When our children read independently, we want them to come to us when they encounter a word they don't understand.

To build your child's vocabulary, expose them to a variety of different words through conversation and reading.

Activities to Support Vocabulary Building

Begin with the basics

Ensure your child can use simple opposites (up/down, big/small), use pronouns correctly (she/her, him/his, they/them, I/me), understand time words (today/yesterday, now/later), use plurals (child/children, person/people) and name simple colours, shapes, letters and numbers.

Introduce new words incidentally through conversation

Look for opportunities in everyday life to introduce new words. For example, "The shirt you're wearing today is aqua. Aqua is a colour that is a bit like blue and a bit like green. This vase on the dining room table is aqua coloured too. Can you think of anything else that is aqua coloured?"

Practise Makes Perfect

Continue to use new words often in the days and weeks following, to reinforce meaning and demonstrate how to use them.

Books

When reading books, point out words and explain their meaning. Use the word in a sentence and have your child come up with a sentence of their own. For example, "This word is imitate. It means to copy someone or something. You imitate your dance teacher when you copy the steps she teaches you."

Word of the Day

Each day, introduce a new word just for fun. Talk about what it means and practise using it in sentences throughout the day. Keep a whiteboard or large piece of butcher's paper on the wall and record the words you've introduced to create a word bank.

Engage in new activities or experiences.

Adding activities which are outside the realm of your child's normal day are a sure-fire way to bring up new words. Activities like fishing, bushwalking, camping or beach trips provide lots of opportunities for vocabulary development.

Importance of Play for Vocabulary

Imaginative play is something very special which should be encouraged. It has many marvellous benefits. It strengthens your child's social and emotional development, encourages creativity, develops problem solving abilities and supports speaking and listening skills. These benefits will be talked about in more detail in the chapter about play. As children engage in imaginative play, they often take on the roles of adults. On Monday they might play mums and dads, on Tuesday teachers and on Wednesday vets. As they adopt these roles, they often use more advanced language or ways of speaking. They'll often try out tricky words during imaginative play as they imitate what they hear from adults. It provides them with opportunities to communicate with others and practise their speaking skills in an environment that is fun and free of pressure.

Make room in your day for meaningful, play-based literacy experiences. Be guided by your child's interests and remember to make it fun. Play with words, dive into books and talk about a variety of subjects. Early literacy skills are the key to future success.

Children need opportunities to explore and play with numbers in situations which are meaningful and fun.

Chapter Two

Early Numeracy Skills

Numeracy is the ability to understand and use mathematics in daily life. Often when we think of numeracy, we think only of numbers and counting, however it is so much more. Children use their knowledge of maths when they identify shapes in their environment, sort their toys by size or colour, or create patterns using buttons. When they use words like *over*, *under* or *beside*, they're demonstrating their knowledge of location. They use measurement knowledge when they classify and compare objects using words like *longer*, *shorter*, *heavier* and *lighter*, or describe time periods as *long* and *short*.

Embedding numeracy in your child's day should be incidental, real world and most importantly, fun. It should involve lots of play, lots of hands-on activities and lots of quality conversations.

Number Sense

Let's begin our journey into numeracy skill development with a concept called number sense. What's that, you may ask? Number sense is the ability to understand numbers and use them flexibly. A child in Kindergarten with good number sense will be able to identify numbers and name them. They will have one-to-one correspondence when counting and understand that numbers represent particular quantities. For example, they can count three items in a box, move three spaces on a board game or jump three times on the spot. A child with number sense understands that numbers go in order. For example, number two always comes after number one. When counting, a child with number sense understands that the last number said tells us how many objects there are altogether. They will also understand that higher numbers represent larger quantities.

So, how do we develop number sense at home? Numbers and counting are a part of our daily lives. When you model using numbers in front of your child, or talk about numbers with them, you're supporting their development of number sense. Children need opportunities to explore and play with numbers in situations which are meaningful and fun. Think games, hands-on materials and real-life situations - no textbooks or worksheets required. Just as reading fluency comes with practise, so does number fluency. To become confident in understanding and working with numbers, children need opportunities to encounter them daily.

Activities to Develop Number Sense

Counting and Number Recognition

One of the earliest steps your child will take towards developing number sense is learning to count. Children experiment with counting from a young age and parents will often hear their children *pretending* to count. For example, a young child may remember and recite number names, *One, two, three, four, five*, before they understand that those number names represent quantities. When teaching number symbols and names it is often tempting to whip out the flash cards. While flashcards are effective at committing number symbols and names to memory, we must ensure that children have a true understanding of what these symbols mean. Providing lots of hands-on counting opportunities with concrete materials first is essential. We want children to master counting with one-to-one correspondence before we worry about number symbol recognition. A really simple and effective activity to promote this skill is having children place objects into an ice cube tray as they count. Provide a bowl of small objects like beads, counters or marbles. Model placing one object into a space while saying the number name. Support your child to have a turn, prompting them to place only one item in each space and say the number name only after the object has been set down. It's very common for young children to try and place multiple objects in a space or say more than one number name at a time so some gentle reminders from you might be needed to ensure any misconceptions are corrected.

Once children have mastered counting concrete objects with one-to-one correspondence and are demonstrating an understanding of what these number names mean, the formal symbols can then be introduced. A really simple activity to help children link the number symbols with quantities is to write the number symbols on clear plastic cups and have children place the correct quantity of objects into the cup. You can introduce the number names by saying, "This is the symbol for number one. Let's put one counter into the cup." The clear cups are really helpful in allowing your child to physically see how many objects have been placed into each cup.

Once children are counting with one-to-one correspondence and beginning to recognise number symbols, lots of real life and play-based situations are needed to reinforce their skills and knowledge.

Count Often with Your Child.

Count the washing as you hang it, the number of apples you put into a bag at the fruit shop or the number of times you pass a ball to one another. Aim for frequent practise in meaningful situations.

Count While Reading

Count the number of letters in words as you read.

Set the Table

Ask your child to set the table for family dinner and help them to work out the number of forks, knives, cups and placemats they will need.

Get Outside

Count objects in the natural world. Collect shells on the beach and count them, count the number of dogs in the park or the number of flowers on a bush.

Threading

Place beads onto pipe cleaners and count each bead as it is threaded. You can place different amounts of beads on each one and talk about which pipe cleaners have more or less beads.

Sing Counting Songs Together

Children's counting songs are catchy (you'll likely find yourself singing them at work), which is why they're so effective for helping children remember the order and names of numbers.

Read Counting Books Together

One is a Snail Ten is a Crab is a fantastic counting book which focuses on counting the number of legs of various animals It also provides a great way to introduce addition as it features different combinations of animals together. For example, a dog has four legs, a snail has one, together they have five legs. Counting books provide a fantastic way to tie in reading and numeracy together and provide opportunities for counting which are entertaining and meaningful.

Spot Numbers in the Wild

Numbers are everywhere; on letter boxes, on signs, in books, on number plates, packets at the grocery store or table numbers in a restaurant.

Create a Number Hunt

Tape numbers around the house or yard and go on a scavenger hunt. Incorporate movement by inviting your child to complete an action when they find each number. For example, five star jumps when they spot number five.

Play Board Games

These are fantastic for consolidating one-to-one correspondence and linking numbers to quantities.

Play Matching Games

Games that require your child to match picture cards with number symbols assist in consolidating number symbols and quantities.

Magnetic Numbers

Use magnetic numbers to put numbers in order. Mix them up and challenge your child to place them in the correct order. Buy a large set containing multiple amounts of each number and challenge them to sort the numbers. You can leave it open by simply asking them to sort all of the numbers, or focus on one number at a time. For example, "I want you to find all the number fives."

Classify Collections of Items as More or Less

Provide a collection of objects, for example, red apples and green apples. Ask your child to count both kinds of apples and identify which colour has more or less.

Practise Forming Number Symbols

Once your child is able to count small quantities, and understands that numbers represent quantities, number formation can be introduced. Provide opportunities for number formation just as you would for letter formation. When writing or tracing numbers, ask your child to draw quantities to match. For example, "Can you draw five cats next to the number five symbol?" This helps to reinforce that important link between symbols and quantities.

Snap

Playing Snap with a deck of cards is a great way to reinforce number recognition by matching number pairs.

Subitising

Subitising is being able to look at a group of objects (up to five) and instantly knowing how many objects there are, without needing to count them. Think of a dice, when we roll the number five we instantly recognise the configuration of dots, without needing to count. Subitising is an important skill in developing number sense. Firstly, it helps to reinforce the connection between number name and quantity. Secondly, it helps children to make connections about how numbers work. For example, when we look at the formation of number five on a dice we see the parts *four* and *one* or when looking at number four we see the parts *two* and *two*.

Activities for Subitising

Subitising Ladybugs

Construct ladybugs out of card and paper, or paint rocks to look like them. Draw or paint the lady bugs to show numbers one to five in the dice configurations.

Play Board Games

A dice is the perfect tool for teaching subitising. When playing board games your child will be exposed to the one to five number formations over and over again.

Set a Challenge

Use your dice or ladybugs to challenge your child to recognise numbers as fast as they can. Flash the ladybug or dice up and ask them to identify the number. Remember, this should be fun and free of pressure.

Simple Addition and Subtraction

Beginning simple addition and subtraction will support your child to understand numbers and how they work. They will learn how to be flexible in the way they use numbers and strengthen their knowledge of bigger and smaller. When beginning addition and subtraction we want to make it as hands-on as possible and introduce it using everyday activities. At this stage there is absolutely no need to introduce formal addition and subtraction symbols. It is important to ensure children have a solid understanding of the concept before symbols are introduced. Addition and subtraction should be introduced using concrete materials and lots of talking. Keep it simple and authentic.

When I introduce addition for the first time, my goal is for my students to understand that when we add numbers together, we make a bigger number. Aim for teachable moments in your child's day. Spot addition happening in real life and talk about it with them. For example, when you are hanging washing on the line, you could peg three socks and ask your child to count them. Peg one more sock on the line and have them tell you how many socks there are altogether. Provide lots of practise with concrete materials and model the skill yourself.

Often when young children arrive at the wrong answer when working out an addition problem, it is due to a counting error. We want to work on the skill of being able to count on from any given number as these addition errors often come about when children count the whole collection, rather than counting on from the beginning number. Counting on is a skill that needs to be modelled and explained. You might say, "In front of me I have three toy cars in my box. I am going to add two more toy cars to the box. I don't want to count all of the cars again, so I am going to lock the number three in my brain and count on. Three…four, five. I now have five cars in my box. Can you count them for me and check there are five?"

I like to introduce addition first. Once I can see that my students have grasped the concept, I'll begin to introduce subtraction. I explain that subtraction means to *take away* and that our number is going to get smaller. Food can be a great way to introduce subtraction. Next time you give your child a small number of food items, use these to model subtraction. For example, "You have four grapes in your bowl. Eat one and tell me how many are left?"

Remember, addition and subtraction are big concepts. They require lots of practise and consolidation. By exposing them to addition and subtraction at a young age, you are building their confidence and setting them up for success later on. It is entirely normal for children to use their fingers when counting on.

Activities for Addition and Subtraction

Make it Hands-on

Use hands-on materials like buttons, counters and toys to model addition and subtraction. For addition, I find it makes the concept clearer when we use two different colours for the parts. For example, start with two red teddy bears and add one blue one. For subtraction, I like to have a designated place, like a bowl or even a chalk circle to place the items I am taking away. This makes it easier to see the remainder.

Play Board Games Using Two Dice

This is really helpful for practising counting on, as your child will need to work out the total number in order to decide how many spaces they need to move on the board.

Draw Pictures to Show Addition and Subtraction

For subtraction, cross out the amount being taken away or cover them with post-it notes.

Create Addition and Subtraction Stories and Draw Them

Tell your child a story that incorporates addition or subtraction. For example, "On a dark and stormy night there were four bats hanging in a dark spooky cave. Can you draw the bats for me?" Allow time for your child to create their drawing before continuing the story. "Later that night two magical, rainbow-coloured bats came into the cave to sleep. Can you draw those bats for me?" Once your child has created their masterpiece ask them to tell you how many bats there are in the cave altogether.

Use the Language of Addition and Subtraction

For addition, use words like *add, altogether, more, how many are there now?* and for subtraction use *take away, less, how many are left?* Don't be afraid to expose your child to the correct mathematical terms of addition and subtraction to build their vocabulary.

Sing Subtraction Songs

The Five Little Ducks and *Ten Little Monkeys* are songs which use addition and subtraction.

Sorting

Sorting is an important skill. It requires children to observe and notice properties like colour, texture or material. It helps them to make distinctions about what makes objects similar or different, and make size comparisons that help to classify items as bigger or smaller. Sorting requires your child to problem solve and encourages the development of thinking skills. Sorting activities can involve handling small objects, making it a great fine motor activity, as well as a speaking task when children are encouraged to verbally explain how they chose to sort their objects.

Provide your child with a variety of objects to sort, both man-made and natural. In my Prep classroom I kept a box of materials for sorting, which included things like coloured counters, plastic animal figures, buttons of various shapes and sizes, shells, dried leaves, laminated pictures of objects, coloured pegs, different sized pom-poms, and beads. Take time to listen to your child's explanations as they justify their sorting criteria. Offer your own suggestions and model different ways of doing things.

Activities for Sorting

Talk About Similarities and Differences

Observe items together and talk about what makes them the same and different. Point out attributes like size, shape, colour and texture.

Find Similar Items

Encourage your child to find things that are the same. For example, you could provide a collection of buttons of different varieties and ask your child to find buttons that they think are the same – ask them to explain why. Model finding similarities yourself and explain. For example, "Well done, you sorted by colour. You put all of the red buttons together. I'm going to put these buttons together because all of them feel soft, they're all made from fabric, that's what makes them the same."

Practise, Practise, Practise

Provide regular opportunities to sort a variety of different items and spends lots of time talking.

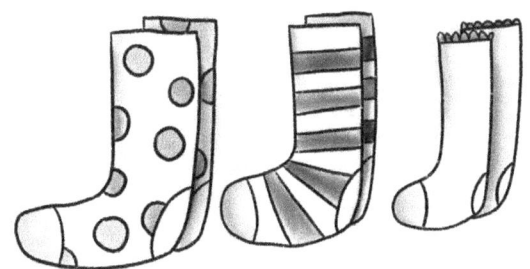

Patterns

In order to identify patterns, copy them and create them, children must be able to recognise attributes like shape, size and colour. These skills can be developed through sorting, which is why I teach that first. As children progress through school, they will learn more complex patterns involving number rules like, *add two each time* and even further down the track, algebra.

In Prep, we first focus on *AB patterns*. These are simple patterns with one rule. For example, *red, blue, red, blue* or *star, circle, star, circle*. Children must be able to identify and copy patterns before they are able to create their own. When introducing patterns, create a simple pattern and read your pattern to your child. For example, "Red butterfly, blue butterfly, red butterfly, blue butterfly, red butterfly, blue butterfly." Provide lots of opportunities to look at, and talk about, patterns.

Activities for Patterns

Model and Explain

Create patterns and talk about them with your child. Modelling and explaining is a great first step. Once they're able to identify patterns and the rule, challenge them to create their own simple patterns. Always ask your child to read their pattern once it is complete. This will help them to identify any errors and also build good habits when it comes to checking their completed work.

Patterns in Our World

Look for patterns in the real world. They're everywhere - tiles in the bathroom, a brick wall, the wings of a butterfly or a colourful dress

Copy Patterns

Provide opportunities for your child to continue patterns you have made. Create a simple pattern and ask them to finish it. Remember to keep it simple - stick to just one rule at the beginning. Once they're confident, create a more complex pattern, for example, red, red, blue, red, red, blue, and ask your child to copy your pattern.

Use Movement

Create patterns using movement. Have your child move their body to create a pattern, for example, hop, jump, hop, jump.

Create Patterns

Provide fun opportunities for your child to create their own patterns. Use things like beads and string, stamps, stickers, paint stencils, Lego or small toys.

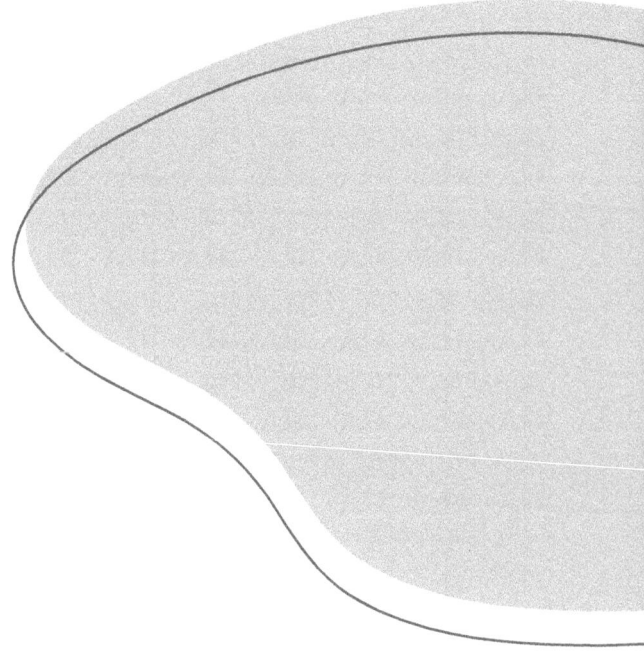

Measurement: Length, Mass and Capacity

In the early years of school, children learn to measure length, mass and capacity using informal units. Items such as paddlepop sticks or toothpicks are laid against desk legs to discover how long they are. Cups of sand or water are used to find out the capacity of a larger object like a jug or bowl. Children guess how many cups of sand might fit inside something, or how many toothpicks long something might be, before heading off to find out. Rather than recording in centimetres, grams or millilitres they might record as __ *paddlepop sticks long* or *holds __ cups of sand*. You can easily provide hands-on experiences for length, mass and capacity at home with household items.

Children need to physically see, hold and fill items to be able to compare them and classify them as longer or shorter, heavier or lighter, or decide which container can hold the most. When introducing length, mass and capacity we need to first ensure our children understand the required language and are able to use it. For length, ensure your child understands the words longer and shorter and for mass ensure they understand the words heavier and lighter. For capacity, you will talk about which item holds the most or can fit the most inside it.

When showing children how to measure, it's important to teach them how to do so with accuracy. Once, while my class was investigating capacity in the sandpit, I overheard a conversation two boys were having. They were both measuring the capacity of the same item, a large yoghurt container, using a plastic cup. One boy said his yoghurt container could hold 10 cups of sand while the other said his could hold 30 cups of sand. As

I watched, I noticed the boy with the higher number of cups wasn't filling his cup all the way to the top each time. Each cup held a different amount of sand. Some filled to the top, others filled less than halfway. It was at this point that I stopped the lesson. I demonstrated filling the cup right to the top to ensure that each one was the same.

Accuracy when Measuring

- When measuring or comparing length, ensure your child is measuring from the very start of the object and placing objects side by side when comparing.
- When comparing the mass of objects and classifying as heavier or lighter, ensure your child is holding the objects at the same time - one in each hand.
- When measuring capacity, if using cups of water or sand, teach your child to fill the cup to the brim so each cup holds the same amount.

Activities for Measurement

Compare household objects

Provide opportunities for your child to compare the lengths and mass of items in your home. Ask questions like, "Which do you think is longer - the teaspoon or the tablespoon?" or, "Which is heavier - the apple or the mango?" Allow time for your child to guess first before measuring.

Measure a Range of Objects

Use different sized containers for capacity. Provide a range of containers like yogurt tubs, buckets, bowls, cups and jugs, and allow your child to compare which items hold the most. Set up a station with water or use sand from a sandpit. Support your child to make comparisons by asking questions like, "Which container holds more cups of sand - the bucket or the bowl?" Help them to fill the containers and count the number of cups it can hold. Provide items like toothpicks, straws and string to measure and compare length.

Measurement: Time

Time can be a tricky concept for young children to grasp. You'll often hear them complaining that they've been waiting for hours when it's only been a few minutes, or they'll proudly tell you that their birthday is next week when in fact it's still months away. It's not surprising really. How often do we say to a child, "Just give me a second please," when what we really mean is five minutes?

We can begin to develop an understanding of duration of time by having conversations with our children about how long things take. You can start by asking your child to tell you something that takes a short time and a long time. By asking this question you can gauge their current understanding of time. Ask questions like, "What do you think takes longer? Taking the dog for a walk or brushing your teeth?"

Adults use the word minute all the time when speaking to young children, with the assumption that they understand what it means. In order for children to grasp the concept of a minute, they need to experience what one minute feels like. A great way to do this is to use a timer. You can also set challenges like, "How many star jumps can you do in one minute?" or, "How many times can you run around our backyard in one minute?"

Throughout your day, talk to your child about how long things take. For example, "That movie went for one hour" or, "It took fifteen minutes to drive to Grandma's house." This helps them to begin developing an awareness of time and exposes them to the language of time.

Starting your day with a really simple calendar is a great way for children to make connections between the days of the week and their own lives. A small whiteboard provides an easy visual reminder. Using a permanent marker, I write sentence starters which I use daily. These are:

- Today is _____
- Tomorrow is _____
- Yesterday was _____
- The weather is _____
- On _____ I _____

For example, *Today is Monday. Tomorrow is Tuesday. Yesterday was Sunday. The weather is cloudy. On Monday I go to dance class.* Completing this each morning helps your child to learn the days of the week and connect them with events in their weekly routine. Help your child to understand the difference between weekdays and weekends.

Shape

Introducing shape can be really fun. To learn shapes, children need to look at them, talk about them, build them and sort them. When I introduce a shape, I like to talk about what makes it special. For example, "This is a square. It has straight sides. Let's trace the sides and count them." I like to spend time introducing each shape, one at a time before I move onto sorting them.

Activities for Shape

Make Shape Posters

Introduce a shape and draw the shape's outline for your child to colour. Talk about the shape's properties and write them on the poster. For example, "Triangle: I have three straight sides." You can display these at home to refer back to,

Build Shapes

Draw shapes on pieces of card or paper and laminate them. These can be used as visual guides and templates to assist your child as they build shapes out of playdough.

Shape Stations

Provide your child with paint, trays of rice or shaving cream, paper and felt pens, or chalk. Using the laminated shape pictures, give your child opportunities to draw shapes using different mediums.

Spot Shapes in the Real World

On a walk, in your home or at the park, look for shapes. You could spot them in the car, for example, circles on the traffic lights, rectangles for street signs and a triangle for a give way sign.

Shape Hunt

Tape pictures of shapes around your home or yard and send your child off to hunt for them.

Shape Sorting

Use shape blocks or cut out pictures and ask your child to sort them using their properties. This provides a great opportunity for conversation about their attributes. Ask questions like, "Why did you put these shapes together? How did you know they were all triangles?"

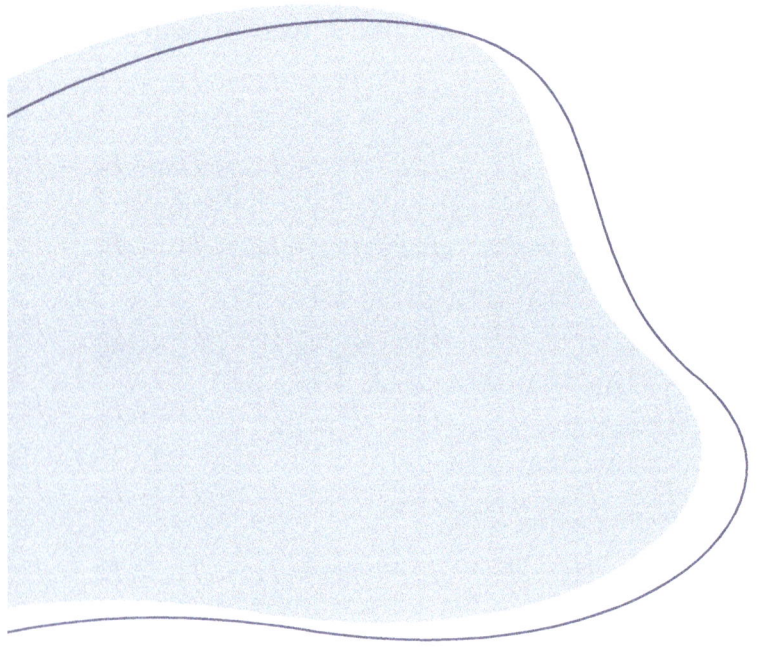

Position and Location

We can begin to introduce the language of position and location throughout our day. Talk about the position of objects at home. For example, "The dog is sitting next to the table," or, "Your toy box is between your bed and cupboard."

Introduce positional words like:

- above, below
- behind, in front of
- beside
- between
- near, far
- on, under

For children to acquire problem solving skills, they must first encounter situations that are challenging.

Chapter Three

Problem Solving Skills

Problem solving skills are important. When a problem arises, we draw on our knowledge and our past experiences to find a solution. Adults use problem solving skills every day and so do children. For adults, problem solving skills might be used to complete tasks at work, to create a household budget or for managing work/life balance Whereas for children, they might be used to put together a jigsaw puzzle or negotiate the rules of a game.

For children to acquire problem solving skills, they must first encounter situations that are challenging. Problem solving requires persistence. Adults can find it difficult not to step in and save the day when they observe children in tricky situations, especially if the child is showing signs of frustration. When children engage in play, many challenging situations arise which call for problem solving skills. This is one of the many reasons that play is so beneficial in the early years of life.

Let's imagine a child is trying to build a sandcastle at the beach using soft, dry sand. After a number of attempts you can see the frustration building. Your instincts are telling you to go over there, fill that bucket with wet sand and create the perfect sandcastle for them. When our children encounter challenges, our role should be to guide, not fix. We can ask careful questions and provide hints that can lead them to a solution. Here are some examples:

- "Why do you think the sandcastle keeps falling down?"
- "Let's try again a different way. How can we change the sand to make the castle stronger?"
- "This is dry sand and this is wet sand. Hold some dry sand in your hand and scrunch it. Now hold some wet sand and scrunch it too. What do you notice about the wet sand when you scrunch it in your hand?"

When you come across problems in your day, talk to your child about the problem and model steps to solve it. Think aloud as you solve the problem:

4. Define the problem: "What is the problem?"
5. Think of solutions: "I could…"
6. Assess the consequences of each solution: "What would happen if…?"
7. Put the solution into practice.
8. Reflect: "What worked well? What didn't?"

Remember to provide lots of praise and reassurance. Children need to feel safe to make mistakes and to get things wrong in order to develop their problem solving skills. Remember to reflect once the problem has been solved. Talk about what worked and what didn't.

Activities for Problem Solving

Provide Open Ended Toys

Open ended toys are versatile and can be played with in lots of different ways. Some examples are animal figurines, dolls, Lego, magnetic tiles, blocks, collage and craft materials, and playdough.

Puzzles

Puzzles are fantastic for developing problem solving skills. Children are required to think deeply as they sort pieces by their attributes and match pieces that fit together.

Construction

Provide materials for your child to use for construction. Blocks and Lego are great, as are household items. Children have wild imaginations; I've seen dollhouses constructed using books, a city made out cardboard boxes and a flower garden made from patty papers.

Block Towers

Challenge your child to stack blocks to make the tallest tower they can.

Ask Open Ended Questions

For example, "What could we use these cardboard boxes to make?" or, "How many different things could we make using these blocks?"

Talk About Problems When You Read Books

Children's books almost always contain a problem which must be solved. When you reach the problem, pause, talk about what the problem is and ask your child to brainstorm ways the character could fix their problem.

Guess Who

This game is terrific for problem solving. It provides lots of opportunities for children to practise asking questions as well as examining clues to solve a problem.

Curiosity is the driving force behind learning. For our children to be motivated learners, they must also be curious learners.

Chapter Four

Nurturing Curiosity

Children are curious creatures. They have vivid imaginations and love to ask why. Curiosity is the driving force behind learning. For our children to be motivated learners, they must also be curious learners. We don't need to *make* our children curious; they are born that way. What we need to do is protect and nurture that curiosity.

My favourite way to spark curiosity is to take children outside. When children are given the opportunity to explore and play in nature, they take an interest in animals, plants and weather. They learn to observe and ask questions. The school where I work has a truly magical nature play area filled with trees and bushes. Fallen branches litter the floor (providing the perfect materials for constructing cubbies) and creepy crawlies dwell in the leaf litter. At the end of each term, when assessment was complete, my class and I would head down to the nature play area. After a quick refresh of the rules to ensure safety and respect for the living things who call the area home, my students were free to explore. Every few minutes, from every direction, I'd hear the words, "Mrs Murray, come quick." I'd rush over to observe something marvellous that someone had spotted - an ant carrying another ant, the shell of a bird's egg or a stink bug - and watch the curiosity ignite. We'd arrive back at the classroom with a list of questions and observations to discuss. A little boy came across an exciting creature once. I wasn't sure if it was a centipede or millipede, so we snapped a photo and examined it together on the classroom whiteboard. We compared it with photographs of both creatures before arriving at the conclusion that it was a millipede.

Nurturing curiosity can be messy, it can be noisy, and it can feel chaotic. We are led by our children, and we follow their interests. If your child asks a question you don't know the answer to, don't be afraid to tell them you don't know. Try saying, "I don't know the answer to that question. Let's find out together."

Activities to Nurture Creativity

Get Outside

Explore the backyard or a local park or beach, go for a walk or a hike, visit a national park or community garden.

Be Guided by Your Child

Follow their interests and support them to find out about them. For example, if your child asks questions about butterflies, visit your local library and find an information book, or look for information online.

Encourage Pretend Play

Children learn about the world around them when they engage in pretend play. As children play, they explore, discover, question and imagine.

Ask Questions

Model curiosity. For example, you could ask the question, "I wonder why butterflies have brightly coloured wings?" Listen to your child's ideas and conduct research to find out about things together.

Try New Foods

Expose your child to new and different foods. Try a food from another culture or head to the fruit shop and select a fruit your child has never tried before. Ask your child to predict what it might taste like before they try it.

Set Up Sensory Play

Select items that feel, look, sound and smell different and allow your child to explore. Try trays of shaving cream or slime, beads, ice cubes, scented playdough, sand, shells, soft and rough fabrics, or even cooked and uncooked pasta. Allow time for exploration.

Play allows children to practise new skills and make mistakes in an environment that is safe and free of pressure.

Chapter Five

The Magic of Play

When children play, they learn. In early childhood education, facilitating carefully planned, play-based learning experiences is a priority. Why? Because they work. As children play, they make sense of their world. They learn new ways of doing things, acquire skills and widen their vocabularies. They face challenges, learn to resolve conflicts and develop emotional intelligence and empathy. They experience joy and disappointment, dare to take risks, and become more resilient. Their bodies and minds grow stronger as they engage in activities that support fine and gross motor development.

Play allows children to practise new skills and make mistakes in an environment that is safe and free of pressure. When we step into children's play, we need to understand our role; we don't want to lead or control. Instead, we want to guide, support, and extend. Allow your child to control the direction of the play and follow their interests. Talk with them about their play, ask questions to stimulate thinking and share information to expand their understanding.

Types of Play

Play comes in many forms. Each type of play is valuable and provides many benefits for children. Children need frequent opportunities to engage in different types of play. Prioritise time for play every day.

Physical Play

When children engage in physical play, they explore movement. They run, jump, climb, dance and hop. They complete obstacle courses, master the monkey bars, create dance routines, and learn to throw and catch. As children participate in physical play they develop their gross motor skills, improve coordination, and grow stronger.

Activities to Support Physical Play

- Visit playgrounds with your child
- Teach ball skills
- Create obstacle courses in your backyard
- Play Hopscotch
- Dance
- Provide time for your child to run and move in wide open spaces
- Teach clapping games

Imaginative Play

Imaginative play, or pretend play, is when children step into different roles or characters and act out situations from a real or fantasy world. This might look like playing shop, pretending to be a fantasy creature or having an elaborate conversation on a pretend phone. Children engage in imaginative play alone or with others. They act out scenarios they have experienced or seen in the past or scenarios they wish to experience in the future.

We spoke earlier about the importance of imaginative play for vocabulary development and speaking skills. Children often mimic adults as they engage in this type of play so it's not unusual to hear complex words and sentence structures being tried out. To my surprise, I once overheard a Prep student uttering the words, "That's simply unacceptable!" as he spoke into a toy iPhone he had constructed from card.

There is something really magical about watching children engage in imaginative play. They have vivid imaginations and fascinating ideas. They're free of inhibitions and their creativity isn't stifled by logic, which means that their play often takes fascinating twists and turns. One moment they're a school teacher teaching a reading lesson, the next they're whisked away to explore a planet in outer space. If only real life was as enthralling as a child's mind dreamed it to be. Imaginative play is a powerful tool for supporting the development of creativity as children create fantasy creatures and worlds or act out scenarios that could never be possible in real life.

When children engage in imaginative play with others, they develop their social skills, begin to develop empathy, understand emotions, practise their communication skills and learn conflict resolution. Playing with others helps children to learn that everyone has different ideas. It puts them into situations where they are required to compromise, to listen to others and share. They begin to learn that they don't always get what they want and that the role of leader is one that must be shared. The first time their idea for play isn't chosen, or others disagree with the way they want to do things, a meltdown may erupt. However, children quickly learn that for play to continue, their emotions need to be controlled. Disappointing and frustrating situations will occur frequently during play, and children will become better at managing their feelings and reactions.

Activities to Support Imaginative Play

Read and Tell Stories

Exposing children to a variety of characters, settings and problems gives them ideas for play scenarios.

Props

Provide props like dress-ups, stuffed toys, dolls, a home corner, pretend household items, a doll house, real life items that are no longer in use (like an old laptop that no longer works) and props or costumes that relate to jobs (like a toy stethoscope or a police uniform).

Encourage Your Child's Interests

Find out what your child is interested in. If it's castles, help them to construct one from old boxes or if they love going to the cinemas, help them to set up a pretend movie theatre at home.

Cubbies

Cubbies make a perfect rainy-day activity and all you need is a table, a sheet and some cushions to make it cosy.

Puppets

Puppets are perfect for inspiring imaginative play and children love them. If you're feeling creative, you might even like to make them with your child.

Manipulative Play

Manipulative play is when children change, move or build with objects. Constructing with Lego or blocks, playing with playdough, making arts and crafts, playing with musical toys and playing in a sandpit are all examples of manipulative play.

Manipulative play inspires creativity, develops problem solving skills and improves fine motor skills.

Activities to Support Manipulative Play

Construction

Provide a range of construction materials like Lego, blocks, carboard boxes and other recycled items.

Nature

Provide time for your child to build with objects in nature. For example, building a cubby using branches. Teach your child to respect the environment by talking to them about the importance of using only broken branches and leaving the homes of animals as you found them.

Arts and Craft

Provide materials for free choice art, craft and collage. Look for materials, both man-made and natural, in an array of colours, sizes and textures.

Musical Instruments

Provide musical instruments and toys that make sounds. You can make simple instruments like maracas with your child using household items like plastic bottles, tape and rice or pasta.

Bead Jewellery

Help your child to make their own bead jewellery using elastic, string and beads.

Sensory Play

Sensory play allows children to observe, explore and

compare different materials and their properties using their senses. This type of play lends itself beautifully to the development of new vocabulary as children describe how things look, feel, smell, taste or sound. For example, when children play with slime or goop, they might describe it as *cold* or *yucky*. We can acknowledge their suggestions and add our own. You could say, "That's right, the slime does feel cold and yucky. I think it also feels stretchy. Did you know another word for stretchy is elastic? They mean the same thing."

Activities to Support Sensory Play

Explore Materials

Provide opportunities for children to play with a range of different materials, like shaving cream, sand, slime and playdough. You can create a sensory bin at home for your child to explore. Fill a tub with a range of natural objects like sand, leaves, shells and sticks or hide small toys in a tub filled with rice or sand. Provide tools like spoons or scoops for digging and exploring.

Gardening

Plant a garden or pot plants. Look for plants with unique smells or edible herbs and flowers.

Nature Play

Earlier we spoke about nature play and its amazing benefits for inspiring curiosity. Nature play should be unstructured and allow children to explore the environment freely and safely. Nature play can provide opportunities to teach children about real world issues, like littering. One afternoon in the nature play area a few students came to me horrified about the amount of litter they were seeing. This led to a discussion about littering and its effect on animal's habitats. Seeing an issue like littering firsthand, as opposed to just hearing about it, can be very powerful for young minds.

Games with Rules

When children engage in games with rules they are engaging in structured play. These include sports, board games and playground games like *tag* or *What's the Time Mr Wolf?* Games with rules help children to develop self-control and deal with disappointment. Through playing these sorts of games, children can learn the art of losing gracefully.

Games with rules:

- Duck Duck Goose
- Musical Chairs
- Sleeping Lions (this one is great for a couple of minutes of peace)
- Simon Says
- Snakes and Ladders
- Hide and Seek

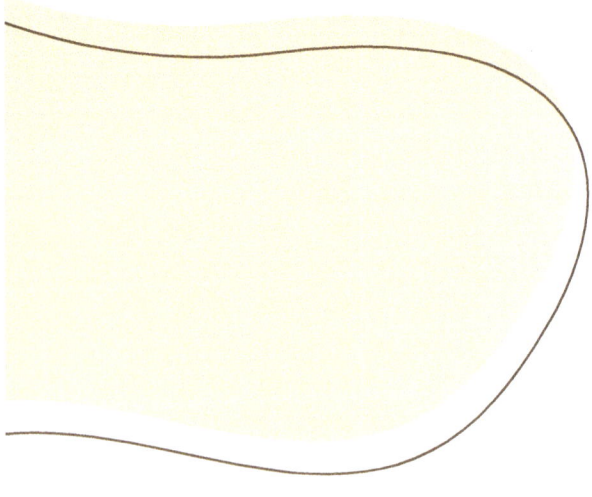

Gross motor skills involve using the large muscles in the body to perform whole body movements.

Chapter Six

Gross Motor Skills

Gross motor skills involve using the large muscles in the body to perform whole body movements. These skills include things like walking, running, standing, jumping and balancing, as well as skills which require coordination like throwing, catching and kicking a ball or using a skipping rope.

An average school day will contain many situations in which gross motor skills will be required. These include tasks like walking to and from the classroom carrying a backpack, sitting upright in a chair or on the carpet, playing on the playground with friends, pushing and pulling chairs in and out of desks and participating in physical education lessons.

To develop gross motor skills, provide lots of opportunities for your child to engage in physical activity.

Activities for Gross Motor Development

Playing on playgrounds

When children use playground equipment they run, jump, hang, climb and balance. They strengthen their muscles and develop coordination.

Hopscotch

Playing hopscotch improves balance and coordination. It also helps in developing spatial awareness as children work out how far they need to jump in order to land in the correct space.

Scooters and Bikes

Riding a scooter or a bike can give children an opportunity to practise balancing. They also strengthen their muscles as they engage them to stay upright and push or pedal.

Obstacle Courses

These are a great way to combine a number of gross motor skills together. Create courses which require children to balance, jump, hop, run, crawl and roll.

Dancing

Whether at home or in a formal class, dancing is a great way to improve coordination and fitness.

Ball Skills

Practise throwing and catching skills using a medium sized ball.

Running

If you're a runner yourself, take your child out for a jog. If you're not so keen on running then you could grab a coffee and head to a park with lots of wide open spaces and set them free while you sit back and watch.

Crossing the Midline

Imagine your body has a line drawn down it which starts at the top of your head and ends between your feet. This line splits your body in half. Crossing the midline is the ability to cross our arms and legs across the middle of our body as we perform a task. For example, when we use our right hand to write, we cross the midline when we start writing on the left side of a page. The ability to cross the midline is developed in childhood and used subconsciously.

Crossing the midline is an important skill used constantly in daily life for tasks like reaching for items, writing, or putting on shoes and socks.

Activities to Support Crossing the Midline

Yoga

Many yoga poses require the skill of crossing the midline. Cosmic Kids Yoga on YouTube is a fantastic resource. It combines storytelling, actions, yoga poses and relaxation.

Simon Says

Incorporate crossing the midline into Simon Says. For example, "Touch your right ear with your left hand."

Playing Tennis or Totem Tennis

When children swing to hit a ball using a tennis racket, they will cross the midline.

Figure Eight

Draw a large figure 8 using chalk or pencil and have your child trace it.

Knowing which learning style works best for your child will assist you in supporting their learning.

Chapter Seven

Catering to Different Learning Styles

Children learn in different ways. Teachers present content in a variety of ways to ensure we reach every child. Knowing which learning style works best for your child will assist you in supporting their learning. Observing your child as they play and learn will give you clues as to what sort of learner they are. There are three main styles of learning; while children can learn from all three styles, they usually favour one.

Visual

People who are visual learners learn best when information is presented visually. They take information in best when they watch someone demonstrate how to do something or look at images. They respond well to colour coded information, mind maps, diagrams and videos.

If your child is a visual learner, they will show an interest in art and drawing. They will pick up new skills faster if they are modelled for them. They also pay careful attention to the pictures when reading a book.

Supporting Visual Learners

- Show don't tell. Demonstrate new skills or show videos when trying to teach something new.
- Create posters with clear pictures and bright colours to present information.
- Provide time for art. Encourage their artistic abilities by providing art supplies.

Auditory

People who are auditory learners learn best by listening. They take in instructions and information best when they are presented orally. Talking through things can be helpful for auditory learners.

If your child is an auditory learner, they will show an interest in music. Auditory learners can often remember and recite songs, rhymes and sayings. They will find following verbal instructions easy.

Supporting Auditory Learners

- Explain how to do things verbally.
- Read to your child and allow opportunities for them to listen to audiobooks.
- Play music.
- Ask them to repeat back instructions you have given.

Kinaesthetic

Kinaesthetic learners learn best through touch and movement. They respond well to learning experiences which are hands-on and prefer to have a go at doing things themselves, rather than hearing or reading about how to do them.

If your child is a kinaesthetic learner, they might like to hold objects in their hands when they look at them. They will be interested in manipulative play and might fiddle often. They love to move and may struggle to sit still for long periods of time.

Supporting Kinaesthetic Learners

- Let them touch or hold things as they observe them.
- Provide manipulative play opportunities and equipment.
- Allow opportunities to act things out.
- Let them have a go at working things out rather than explaining first.
- Provide plenty of outdoor play to burn off excess energy.
- Complete homework in short bursts and allow lots of movement breaks.

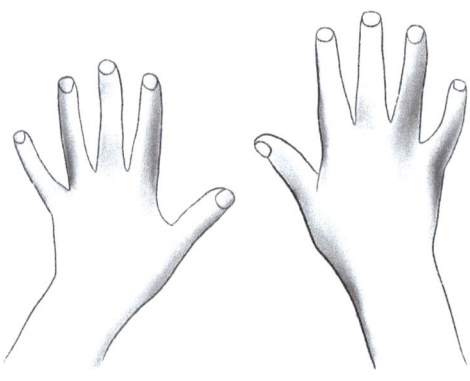

The most important thing to remember when talking about school is to keep it positive.

Chapter Eight

Managing Nerves

Before your child begins school it's important to talk with them about what it might be like. This provides a great opportunity for them to ask questions and also to bring up anything that's worrying them. Uncovering any anxieties they have early on gives you a chance to manage them before they manifest in a big way. You can share stories from your own school experience. Grandparents often love to regale their grandchildren with horror stories from their time at school, but it might be best to save stories of being whacked with the cane and pelted with blackboard dusters for another time. Preferably once your little one is settled into school.

The most important thing to remember when talking about school is to keep it positive. We want to avoid saying things like, "If you don't listen to your teacher you'll get into big trouble." We want to encourage respectful behaviour without instilling fear. When introducing the role of a teacher, introduce them as a safe person; someone your child can go to when they're feeling scared or worried or need help. Be enthusiastic about school. Talk about all the fun things your child will get to do and learn when they get there.

There are lots of wonderful picture books you can read

with your child about starting school. Often the character in the story deals with emotions they may be feeling, like anxiety or fear, and overcomes them.

Books About Starting School
- *The Kissing Hand* by Audrey Penn
- *Starting School* by Janet and Allen Ahlberg
- *First Day* by Andrew Daddo

When children express concerns about starting school (perhaps they're nervous about not having anyone to play with or getting in trouble for breaking a rule) it's important not to discount those feelings. It's tempting to say things like, "Don't be silly, you'll be fine," but that can make children feel as if they shouldn't have those feelings. This means they might be less likely to come to you the next time they feel that way. It's important to acknowledge any feelings they have and work on ways to reassure them or come up with a plan for what to do if the thing they are worrying about happens. For example, your child might say, "I'm worried I'll get lost in the playground at lunchtime." You could say something like, "I understand why you're feeling worried, getting lost is scary. The good news is schools are very busy places. There's always someone around who can help you. Your teacher will spend time showing you where everything is, but if you get lost at lunchtime there will be a teacher on duty. Their job is to make sure all the children are safe at lunchtime. If you're lost, you can ask them to help you. You can also ask one of the other children in your class."

Take your child with you when you shop for school supplies. Selecting a new water bottle or pencil case to take to big school can be exciting and helps build those positive feelings before the first day. Let your child try on their uniform and do a practise run of carrying their school bag.

Most schools hold an orientation session for Prep students where children spend a morning in their new classroom with their teacher. Make attending this session a priority. It's so effective at helping to quell first day nerves. For one, their teacher is no longer just a name. The words *your teacher can help you* become a lot more meaningful when they can put a face to a name. The orientation session will also give them a chance to meet their new classmates. Organising a few playdates before school kicks off will ensure they have a few familiar faces when they step into that classroom on day one.

The night before your child's first day of school make sure their bag is packed and their uniform is laid out ready - the last thing you want is a frantic rush in the morning. Before school, sit down to a healthy breakfast together before leaving. It's a good idea to arrive nice and early on the first day. This gives you and your child plenty of time to mingle with the other children and parents outside the classroom before the bell rings. Once inside, follow the lead of your child's teacher. Some teachers like to invite the parents in for a few moments on the first day to assist with tasks like pinning on name tags, unpacking school equipment and settling. Try not to linger though, a quick goodbye is best. Save the tears for the car (if you can) as your child will be looking to you for confidence and reassurance. Tears on the first day, for children and parents, are very normal. Allow a few days or even weeks for them to settle in. It's a big change for everyone.

If it's been a few weeks and your child is still struggling with separation at drop-off, it might be time to speak with your child's teacher about putting some sort of plan in place. This can look different depending on the child's needs and their teacher. Assigning a job for arrival time is a distraction strategy I've used on many occasions for children experiencing low-level separation anxiety. It can be as simple as helping the teacher assistant to place worksheets on the desks or helping to sharpen pencils. It can be upsetting dealing with separation anxiety and very hard to keep walking towards the door but staying longer can often escalate things. If your child's teacher tells you to go, trust them. Walk out in a calm and confident manner (even if you need to fake it) and don't look back. Your child's teacher is well equipped to handle the situation.

If you and your child's teacher have put a plan in place and things are escalating, not improving, it might be time to seek help beyond your child's classroom teacher. Schools will usually have a guidance officer that both parents and students can access. They can provide support in many forms, whether that's coming to the classroom to observe and assist with settling in, or working with you to put strategies in place for the future. It's best to try and get on top of these things quickly to avoid things escalating and causing severe meltdowns or flat-out school refusal.

Just like children need to learn skills to read, they also need to learn skills to be organised.

Chapter Nine

Independence and Organisation Skills

Parents often view the path to school readiness as a purely academic venture. They want to support their children to be good readers, writers, and mathematicians. This is understandable, these things are important, but we need to remember that academic learning is just one piece of the puzzle. There are many other factors that ensure a child is ready for school. As well as developing skills for learning, we want to develop independence, social skills, emotional maturity and organisation skills.

When children start school, they're required to follow rules and instructions, ignore distractions when completing work, collaborate with others, and take responsibility for their own belongings. It's a lot and it can often come as a shock in week one. We can lessen this shock by teaching basic organisation skills at home. Just like children need to learn skills to read, they also need to learn skills to be organised. Here are just a few things you can do to help support their transition.

Opening Packets and Containers

Morning tea and lunchtime supervision at the beginning of the school year can be chaotic. Coaxing a large group of excited little people to remain seated, keep their hats on and eat their food (healthy first) in an allocated ten minute time frame is no easy task. As teachers walk around reminding children to sit and eat, we are faced with numerous events which seem to prevent them from doing so. Misplaced lunchboxes and water bottles, siblings' lunchboxes with the *wrong sandwich* placed in school bags by mistake, other children *annoying them*, lost hats, sore fingers, dropped sandwiches and anxiety over having no one to sit or play with, just to name a few. While all this is going on, at any given time I will have a line of little ducklings trailing behind me requiring assistance to open various packets and containers. With such a small ratio of teachers to children, some children will spend half of their eating time waiting for a packet or container to be opened.

Children are still developing their fine motor skills and finger strength so opening things like plastic containers, muesli bars and squeezy yoghurts requires some practise. A good trick for squeezy yoghurts is to open it as you place it in the lunch box and screw the lid back on. Children often struggle with breaking the plastic seal as they don't yet have the required finger strength and coordination.

Next time your child is eating a snack which might one day be packed in the school lunchbox, begin teaching them how to open it themselves. Give them plastic containers from the drawer and let them have a go at opening them or explain to them how to tear open a plastic wrapper. While these things seem easy to us, they're skills which often need explicit teaching for our children to master.

I ask the children in my class to ask three [friends] before they ask me. Often there's a packet and container opening expert in the crowd ready to save the day.

Packing Bags and Lunchboxes and Looking After Belongings

In the space of a school week, on average, I receive two emails from parents about lost belongings, pick up six hats, two lunch boxes and a watch left behind on the bag rack (some without names), and send three children to lost property to search for jumpers. Lost belongings can become an incredibly frustrating and expensive battle for parents. Simply telling a child to put their things back in their bag isn't always enough, it's a skill which must be practised.

Getting children involved in packing their own bags can be really helping in building this skill. Next time your child is going for a sleepover at a friend or grandparent's house, work with them to pack the bag. Teach simple skills like folding items to make them smaller, placing larger items on the bottom and small or fragile items on top.

Children often struggle to fit their hat and lunchbox back in their school bag if they've never packed a bag before. This can result in frustration and anxiety which leads to hats or lunchboxes being left out and jumpers strewn across bag racks to later be left behind. The night before school, pack your child's school bag with them. Help them work out a place for their lunchbox, hat and water bottle to ensure everything fits, and show them strategies to fit everything in. Get them involved in the lunch packing process.

Making your child responsible for packing their own bag and lunchbox helps to build independence and will teach them to be responsible for their belongings. Often, I'll hear a dismayed voice utter the words, "Oh no! Mum forgot to pack my hat!" to which my reply is, "Mum didn't forget to pack the hat. It's your hat, not mum's. It is your job to make sure you have everything you need for school." A checklist placed near your child's school bag is a great way to ensure they have everything they need for their day. Laminate it and Blutac it to the wall. As they place each item into their school bag have them tick it off the list using a whiteboard marker. Include a checklist for each day of the week to ensure things like their library bag and homework is packed on certain days as required.

Despite everyone's best efforts, things will inevitably get lost as children are easily distracted. Naming all of your child's belongings is the best way to maximise the chances of things making their way back home again.

An important habit to build is putting things away as soon as they are no longer needed. Children will often leave their things lying around in the classroom when they finish using them. Once, a little girl in my class was reading a special book from home during silent reading time. She left the book on her desk and walked away. Later during free play, another child sat in her desk to draw with a friend. They kindly placed her book on the bookshelf thinking it was a class book. Later, the little girl returned to her desk and found that her book was no longer there. After a quick search of the classroom, I stopped free play to ask if anyone had seen the book. Eventually the book was found discarded in the home corner under the pretend stove. We had a big chat about putting things away in the right spot. This habit can be built at home. When your child is playing with toys or drawing with coloured pencils, remind them to pack up before they begin a new activity and support them to place items back in their correct place.

Before we move on, I'll finish with one last piece of advice about bags - let your child carry their own bag. Yes, it's a little bit heavy, but it's theirs and it's going to be theirs for the next thirteen years so let them get used to carrying it now. I often see parents leaving the school grounds resembling pack horses - three school bags, a soccer ball, and some artwork, while their children race ahead, hands free to the car. Get them used to carrying their bags now while they're light because down the track they could be stuffed full of heavy textbooks. A Prep student is more than capable of carrying a backpack with a hat, lunchbox, and water bottle inside.

Timetables

I like to begin each school day with the calendar followed by a visual timetable. Children thrive on routine and love to know what's happening next. They quickly develop an understanding of events that take place on certain days of the week.

Creating a visual timetable at home can help children to prepare for their day. Some children don't deal well with surprises and like to know what to expect when they show up to school each day.

You can create a set of laminated picture cards to represent events in your child's week and organise these under labels displaying the days of the week. This might include the days your child attends childcare or Kindergarten and any other activities which occur on a weekly basis. Once school begins, include special activities in the school week like library borrowing, PE and assembly. Also include any outside of school activities like soccer practise or dance class. It's a good idea to also create some laminated blank squares to write any special events such as playdates, school dances or sports carnivals with a whiteboard pen. Display the timetable in the area you use for packing bags or in a space in their bedroom.

Getting Dressed

There will be times when children will be required to dress themselves independently at school. For example, they could have an accident and require a change of uniform, or participate in school swimming and need to get changed after the lesson. Provide opportunities for your child to practise getting dressed into their school uniform. Buttoning and unbuttoning buttons takes lots of practise to master, as does putting on shoes and socks. Unless your child is confident with shoelaces, I would suggest buying shoes with Velcro straps and get them used to doing them up.

Packing Up and Tidying

Children are required to pack up and tidy multiple times throughout the school day, usually in a short space of time. They're responsible for keeping their desk area tidy, as well as helping to keep the classroom tidy. Provide lots of practise at home. Ensure your child is responsible for keeping their room clean, as well as packing away anything they use or play with in the house.

Packing up and tidying can be a tiresome activity for both the children and the adult supervising which is why I often turn it into a game. Never have I seen the classroom cleaned so quickly and thoroughly as when I turned it into a game or challenge.

Games for Tidying Up

Beat the Song

I put on a song, it can either be a tidy up song (there are plenty on YouTube) or any song your child loves. I challenge the children to have the classroom tidied before the song ends.

Timer

I display a large timer on the whiteboard and time how fast the class can pack up. The visual is a great motivator. Next time, we try and beat our previous time.

Lucky Rubbish

Lucky Rubbish is a game I use to ensure all the bits and pieces are picked up after an art or craft activity. I tell the children there is one piece of rubbish which is *lucky*. The person who finds it is the winner and gets a sticker or prize. I pick out something that is laying on the floor like a small paper offcut and watch to see which child happens to pick it up. Once the classroom is tidy, I reveal which item was the lucky rubbish and ask the person who found it to stand up. This is perfect for pack up time with more than one child.

Making friends is an important part of school. A few smiling faces at the classroom door each morning can really help in crushing any drop-off jitters your child might be experiencing.

Chapter Ten
Social Skills and Friendships

Making friends is an important part of school. A few smiling faces at the classroom door each morning can really help in crushing any drop-off jitters your child might be experiencing. For some children, collecting friends is effortless. They can talk to just about anyone about anything and feel confident in approaching any social situation and asking to join in. For others, making friends can be a little trickier. Working on social skill development is important, as is teaching children not just how to make friends, but how to keep them.

Playdates and Social Events

Children need lots of time to play and interact with their peers. Playgroup, Kindergarten, trips to a local playground and playdates with friends' children allow for opportunities to socialise and make connections with children of a similar age. As children play, they will undoubtedly experience conflict and a range of emotions. Our role is to teach children to interact appropriately with others and support them to manage their emotions. If your child feels left out or encounters a child who makes them feel sad or unsafe, having you there on the sidelines to step in and help them find their way will provide confidence and comfort. Sometimes simply talking through what happened is all they need. Other times they might need some advice or strategies to help them decide what to do next.

Joining In

Often, we expect our children to just *go and play*. Adults often assume that children will be happy to approach a group of unknown children playing on the playground and join in simply because they're kids. However, this can be a daunting task. Just imagine walking into a bar or restaurant and approaching a group of people you don't know and asking, "Can I sit with you?" The mere thought is enough to make most adults feel faint, yet we expect this of our children.

If your child hangs back and watches as others play, they might need your help. Providing our children with the words they need can be effective. Practising the question, "Could I please join in with your game?" is a good place to start. Sometimes even prompting them to begin with a simple hello or encouraging them to ask another child their name is enough to kick things off.

Social Skills

Modelling and practising social skills at home will be helpful for making friends and interacting positively with other children.

Here are some things you can work on together at home.

Greeting Others

Teach your child to begin a conversation with a simple greeting. Encourage them to use the person's name if they know it.

Using Eye Contact

Provide gentle reminders when you speak with your child. Eye contact is a social skill that some children find difficult or uncomfortable at first.

Using Manners

Create the habit of using words like please, thank you and excuse me when appropriate.

Turn Taking and Sharing

Arguments in the playground often come about because someone is perceived to be not sharing or to be taking over a game. Modelling and reinforcing the importance of these skills at home can be helpful.

Standing Up to Others

There will be times when your child will need to stand up for themselves. The ability to tell another child whose words or actions make them feel uncomfortable or unsafe to stop or leave them alone is an important skill. Standing up to another person, particularly one who is being unkind, can feel scary. Your child might need your support the first few times.

We are not able to protect our children from encountering situations which are anxiety inducing, difficult or challenging. Instead, we must give them the tools to flourish when these situations arise.

Chapter Eleven

Resilience

Resilience is the ability to thrive when challenged, and to face difficult situations head on. A resilient child will approach new and tricky situations with a positive attitude and have the ability to manage their emotions. When things go wrong, a resilient child is able to bounce back. Children are not born with resilience. While some might be more laidback or confident by nature, resilience is something that can be nurtured through supportive relationships and with the teaching and modelling of skills. We are not able to protect our children from encountering situations which are anxiety inducing, difficult or challenging. Instead, we must give them the tools to flourish when these situations arise.

Supportive Relationships

In the classroom, we talk about *safe people*. For a child, a safe person should be someone who they can approach when they need help without fearing judgement. Safe people are a child's safety net; they know their safe people are always there to catch them when they fall. A child surrounded by supportive people will feel more confident to try new things and take risks. Allow your child to speak freely about their feelings, celebrate their achievements and let them know it's okay to make mistakes. Teach your child that mistakes give us opportunities to grow and learn.

For our children to become resilient, we must model resilience ourselves. Be mindful of your own reactions to challenges and disappointment. While we might feel like throwing the new printer out the window when we can't work out how to install it, this behaviour won't help our children on the path to developing emotional resilience. To model resilience, talk to your child about how you're feeling. For example, "I feel disappointed because I made a mistake at work today. It's going to be tricky but tomorrow I'm going to work out a way to fix it." Making our children aware of their emotions, and the emotions of others, will help them to develop empathy.

When our children try to do something tricky and feel like giving up, we need to support them to have another go. Start by acknowledging how they're feeling. For example, "I understand you're feeling frustrated because you can't get the blocks to stack." Then, provide encouragement and help them with another attempt, "Don't give up, let's think of another way to do it and try again together." Developing problem solving skills and resilience go hand in hand.

Optimism and Positive Self-Talk

For children to be resilient, they must be optimistic. We want to develop positive self-talk and instil self-belief. For this to happen, we need to model this ourselves. I was once drawing a picture on the whiteboard during a phonics lesson. We were learning about the letter *h* and I was drawing a horse which turned out to be rather strange and abstract looking. I professed to my class that I was terrible at drawing. A little girl said to me, "No you're not, you just need more practise. That's what my mum says when I think I'm bad at something." My first thought was wow! What a fantastic job this little girl's mother had done at curbing negative self-talk. My second thought was, I need to start practising what I preach. Here I was trying to develop positive self-talk in my students, all the while modelling the opposite. "What a great helper you are," I said. "You are absolutely right, I'm not terrible at drawing, I just need to spend some more time practising to get better. Thank you so much for reminding me."

When our children say negative things about themselves, we can take their words and reframe them. For example, if your child says, "I'm no good at maths," we can say, "You find maths tricky and that's okay. Every time you work on maths your brain gets smarter and you get better at it." Or they might say, "I'll never remember how to write my name." You could respond with, "Learning to write your name is tricky but I know you can do it. It might take time, but I believe in you and I'm here to help." By letting our children know that we believe in them, they will start to believe in themselves. When they master that skill they've been working on, let them know how proud you are of them and celebrate their success.

You can make affirmation cards for your child to help with self-belief. Write positive statements on the cards, decorate and laminate them and read them with your child before bed each night or before school in the morning. Write statements that you would like your child to believe about themselves. For example, *I am kind and a good friend* or *I am clever. Each day I learn new things* and *I don't give up when something is tricky*.

It's Okay to Ask for Help

Whether they're struggling with big emotions or trying to master a new skill, it's important that children understand that it's okay to ask for help. We want our children to be independent and to give things a go on their own, but also know that asking for help is an important skill for learning. Children who know when to ask for help are able to make faster progress in meeting their learning goals. A very capable student in my Year One class blew me away once when she came to me, writing book in hand and said, "I'm happy with my writing but is there anything I can do to make it better?" At such a young age she was already demonstrating such amazing intrinsic motivation, independence and emotional maturity. She knew how and when to ask for help. I stopped my lesson to highlight this amazing behaviour to the rest of the class. Asking for help doesn't have to be reserved only for times when we don't know how to do something, it can also be a powerful tool for self-improvement.

Some children can be reluctant when it comes to asking for help. Some gentle encouragement can assist. If you see them struggling, you could say to them, "I can see you're having trouble with that. Did you need some help?" This can show your child that you're open to help them when they need it. Remind your child that their teacher is also there to help. Provide them with a script if asking adults for help is something they struggle with and have them practise with you at home. Keep it simple and polite, for example, "Mrs Smith, I'm having trouble, could you please help me?"

Encourage Risk Taking

Risks are often thought of as dangerous, however, many risks come with incredible benefits. Taking risks is important for increasing independence, growth and resilience. Providing a safe and supportive environment in which your child feels comfortable to take risks is key. Putting scaffolds in place to support them as they try new things and explore their world will improve their confidence. An example would be teaching your child to ride a bike. You begin with training wheels to get them used to the bike, they work out how to get on and off the bike, to use the pedals and to steer with the handlebars. Once they're confident, you take those training wheels away and support them by keeping your hand on the handlebars. Then one day, as you run alongside the bike, you let go and watch as they take off across the park. Riding a bike is a risk, it can be scary, but with good supports in place it is achievable, and the benefits outweigh the negatives.

When your child feels worried about taking a risk, help them to identify the root of their anxiety. Find out exactly what they're worried about. For example, most children who feel anxious about riding a bike, do so because they know there's a possibility they can fall off and get hurt. Help your child to consider the positives and negatives of a risk before they take it. Sometimes talking about the worst-case scenario can help in reducing anxiety, especially if the worst-case scenario has been inflated or distorted by fear. Defining the positive and negative consequences will help your child to decide if they're ready to take the risk.

Having the confidence to take risks has many benefits for

learning. Children who are confident to take risks will raise their hand to answer questions in class. They understand there is a risk they might get it wrong, but they have the resilience to try again. Risk takers will experiment with new vocabulary in their writing and participate in class discussions without hesitation. When teaching Year Three, we focus on beginning a story in an exciting way - an action word (bang, crunch) or suspense (I swallowed hard, my heart pounding in my chest as I entered the candle lit room.). This was a change for some students who would always begin their story with *one day* or *once upon a time*. Some of my more capable students liked to play it safe. They were only comfortable replicating something similar to the story starters I had modelled. While their sentences were well written, grammatically correct and ticked all the boxes, it was some of my less capable writers who knocked my socks off. Their story starters were exciting and unique and sounded nothing like mine. Why? They were risk takers. They played with words and experimented with new sentence starters without getting bogged down by the fear of getting it wrong. Were their story starters grammatically perfect? No. Were they memorable? Absolutely.

Managing Emotions

Having the capacity to manage emotions is an important part of being resilient. Talking to your child about their feelings is an important first step in developing their ability to recognise them. This can be difficult for young children. Saying things like, "I noticed you were feeling frustrated because you couldn't fix your toy," gives them the language they need to talk about emotions and develops awareness. Talking about your own emotions helps, as does talking about the emotions of characters in books or TV shows. Building up a bank of words your child can use to talk about their feelings is important in developing emotional awareness. Children sometimes struggle to identify their emotions because they are unable to find the right word. Children need to understand that having negative feelings is okay but reacting to these feelings in a destructive way is not. For example, feeling angry about something is okay, but kicking or hitting someone because you felt angry is not. During a social skills lesson with my Year One class, we read a scenario in which a little boy broke another child's toy because he felt angry that they wouldn't let him play with it. I asked the question, "Is it okay for the little boy to feel angry?" and had the children raise their hands to answer yes or no. I was surprised to learn that the majority of the class voted for no - they believed that the little boy was not allowed to feel angry. Negative emotions are often linked with negative actions, which is why children can develop the idea that they are not allowed to feel them. It's important for children to understand that having negative feelings is normal and it's how we react to them that is important.

When we say things like, "It's not a big deal," or, "You're being silly,' we send the message that their emotions are wrong or not allowed. Saying things like, "I know you felt sad that you lost your toy. I feel sad too when I lose things that are special," acknowledges their emotions and make them feel heard. Once they're feeling calmer you can work on a plan together to find a solution. Resilient children are able to identify their emotions and find ways to problem solve. Practising calming strategies such as counting to ten or taking deep breaths can give your child a toolbox to help them ride out the big emotions until they pass.

Remember, you know your child better than anyone.

Chapter Twelve

School Ready Checklist

Use this checklist to identify the skills your child is able to demonstrate and any areas in which they might require some more practise.

Skills for Learning	Yes	Not Yet
Opens a book correctly		
Demonstrates an understating of text direction (left to right)		
Talks about events in stories		
Can use pictures to make predictions or tell a story		
Attempts or pretends to read books		
Can recite the alphabet		
Can recite simple songs and rhymes		
Is beginning to recognise letters		
Is beginning to understand that letter symbols represent sounds		
Can draw circles, dots and lines		
Can draw simple recognisable pictures		
Can recognise and write their own name correctly (uppercase first letter then lowercase)		
Is able to take turns when having a conversation		

Skills for Learning	Yes	Not Yet
Demonstrates whole body listening		
Is able to answer questions		
Speaks in complete sentences		
Uses eye contact and speaks clearly		
Can listen without interrupting		
Can initiate conversations		
Is able to ask for help		
Plays independently and with others		
Recognises and orders numbers 10 and below		
Is able to count small collections of objects with one-to-one correspondence		
Is beginning to understand that numbers represent quantities		
Can sort objects using a simple criterion (colour, size)		
Recognise and name basic shapes (square, circle, triangle, rectangle)		
Draws simple pictures and can talk about them		
Uses simple directional words e.g. Up, down		
Can name basic colours		

Fine and Gross Motor Skills	Yes	Not Yet
Uses a pincer grasp to pick up small objects		
Holds a pencil and attempts correct pencil grip		
Can use a glue stick and scissors		
Is able to open simple containers and unscrew and screw lids		
Can pick up small objects		
Is able to manipulate playdough		
Is able to throw, kick and catch a ball		
Demonstrates balance e.g. Can hop on one leg		
Can manage stairs independently and safely		

Independence and Organisation	Yes	Not Yet
Is able to use the toilet independently		
Can wash and dry hands		
Is able to dress themselves		
Can put on own shoes (Velcro, not laces)		

Independence and Organisation	Yes	Not Yet
Can follow instructions with more than one step e.g. Put away your hat and lunchbox then come and sit down		
Can open a water bottle and lunchbox independently		
Recognises own belongings		
Is able to blow their nose independently.		
Packs and unpacks own school bag		
Attempts to solve problems independently		

Social Skills	Yes	Not Yet
Is able to separate from parents		
Copes when things are different		
Takes turns when playing		
Is able to share and cooperate with others.		
Sits and listens to a story being read		
Greets others		
Initiates or joins in with play		
Uses words to resolve conflicts		
Uses manners unprompted		

Notes:

What Can I Do If I Think My Child Isn't Ready?

Despite even the best efforts of parents, some children are simply not ready. In Queensland, for children to enrol in Prep, they must turn five by the 30th of June of that year. This means a Prep class will be made up of children who are four turning five and others who are five turning six. You can make the decision to delay entry to Prep by one year if you feel that your child is not quite ready. Some children benefit immensely from completing another year of Kindergarten.

Parents choose to delay enrolment to Prep for a range of reasons. This might be because:

- Their child's birthday falls close to June 30. Parents might have concerns about their child being one of the youngest in the class.
- Their child still has separation issues.
- Their child requires support with social skills or emotional regulation.
- Their child requires further fine and gross motor skill development.
- Their child has problems with concentration, listening and impulse control.
- Their child lacks independence or organisation skills.

Delaying entry to Prep is a decision which requires careful consideration. While it is a personal decision, speaking with your child's Kindergarten teacher can be helpful. Remember, you know your child better than anyone so trust your instincts and be confident in your decision.

If at any point you have concerns about your child's development or ability to learn, speak to your child's GP. They will be able to point you in the right direction to have the issue investigated.

At the end of your child's first week of school remember to take some time to celebrate and unwind. The beginning of the school year can be a rollercoaster of emotions.

Chapter Thirteen

Week One and Beyond

You made it! You got them through the door on day one and week one was smooth sailing. So, what's next? Here are a few tips and tricks for the days and weeks following.

Routine, Routine, Routine

Establish a consistent before and after school routine. A morning routine could consist of sitting down to a healthy breakfast, getting dressed into a school uniform, packing belongings for the day, and talking about any special activities or events for the day on the way to school. This will help your child to feel organised for their day. An after-school routine could consist of talking about the school day on the way home or over afternoon tea and unpacking the school bag.

Down Time

A school day is exhausting for your little one. Provide plenty of time for relaxation and play in the afternoon. Once the school bag has been unpacked, let your child unwind and switch off.

Homework and Reading

At the beginning of the school year, teachers usually allow a few weeks for students to settle in before assigning homework. Homework will look different depending on the school or teacher. Generally, in the first year of school, homework will include sightwords and home readers. There may also be tasks assigned online through an app or website. The first year of school is a good time to set up consistent homework expectations. This could include allocating a certain amount of time each afternoon or evening for homework. Remember, children at this age have a short attention span so keep homework activities to fifteen minutes or less. Provide lots of movement or play breaks. Using a timer can be effective. Display the timer and explain to your child that once the timer is finished, they can have time to play. When teaching sightwords you can use many of the activities we spoke about earlier - remember to keep it hands-on and fun. In my opinion, the most important homework is reading. Make time for reading every day.

Other Parents

School drop-off and pickup or school events can be a fantastic time to reach out to other parents in your child's class. Each year it is wonderful to watch the friendships and support network the parents in my class form. From help with last minute school pickups and drop-offs, to reminders about upcoming school events or after school playdates in the local park, my parents have always been there to help each other out. The school year can be busy and at times overwhelming so having some other parents, especially those who have done the school thing before, can be valuable.

At the end of your child's first week of school remember to take some time to celebrate and unwind. The beginning of the school year can be a rollercoaster of emotions. It's an exciting yet exhausting time for both kids and their parents. Spend some time on the weekend doing something special that your whole family enjoys and recharge before that busy second week begins. Give your child and yourself a pat on the back, you did it! And remember, every time you read to, talked to or played with your child you helped them on their way to becoming school ready.

Resources to Support Learning

Below is a list of resources to keep in your home to support learning activities.

General Items

- Beads
- Buttons
- String
- Collage materials
- Coloured pencils, crayons, felt pens, gel pens
- Fabric in different textures
- Chalk
- Pom-poms
- Pegs
- Paint and paintbrushes
- Coloured paper and cardboard
- Glue
- Children's scissors
- Playdough
- Stickers
- Post-it notes

Literacy Specific

- A selection of fantastic picture books (see booklist for ideas)
- Laminated large letters
- Handwriting chart, or poster, showing direction and order of letter formation
- Pencil grip
- Letter magnets

Numeracy Specific

- Counters
- Dice
- Board games
- Number magnets
- Measurement materials (string, cups, different sized containers)
- Shape blocks
- Sorting materials (counters, small toys, buttons, beads, dried leaves, shells, coloured pegs, pom-poms)

Open Ended Toys and Construction

- Puzzles
- Magnetic tiles
- Animal figurines
- Lego
- Wooden blocks
- Carboard boxes

Toys for Imaginative Play

- Home corner and equipment
- Pretend cash register
- Dress-ups

Gross Motor Skills

- Medium sized ball
- Skipping rope
- Hula hoop

Apps and Computer Programs

- Reading Eggs (A reading program for ages 2-13. Covers phonics, phonemic awareness, vocabulary, fluency and comprehension)
- Speech Blubs (A speech therapy app. Aids speech development through games and activities)
- Elmo Loves the 123s (Children learn with Elmo. Number formation and identification, addition and subtraction and counting activities are included)

YouTube

- Jolly Phonics (Actions and songs to teach sounds)
- Jack Hartmann (Learning songs which incorporate movement and actions)
- Super Simple Songs (A range of children's song)
- Cosmic Yoga (Children's yoga taught through storytelling)
- Storyline Online (Popular children's books read by celebrities)

Simple Playdough Recipe

Ingredients

- 2 cups flour
- 1 cup salt
- 1 tbsp oil
- 1 cup cold water
- 1 drop food colouring

*Optional - 2-3 drops of essential oil to make scented playdough, or glitter to make sparkly playdough

Method

1. Combine dry ingredients.
2. Slowly add wet ingredients and mix to combine.
3. Knead well until soft.
4. Add more flour if dough is sticky.

A note about playdough

I recently learnt that playdough is highly toxic to dogs due to the high salt content. We all know how much playdough ends up on the floor so keep an eye out if you've got a furry friend at home.

Rainbow Rice

Equipment

- Rice
- Food colouring in different colours
- Water
- Ziplock Bags

Method

1. Place one cup of rice into a Ziploc bag. The amount of rice and bags needed will depend on how many colours you plan to make. I usually do five colours.
2. Mix one teaspoon of water with 20 drops of food colouring and place into bag.
3. Close bag and shake until colour has coated all the rice evenly.
4. Place coloured rice onto baking paper to dry.
5. Repeat for each colour.
6. Once dry, pour rice together into a plastic tub and shake to mix.

Thank you

To you, the reader. Thank you so much for reading. I know firsthand how busy parents can be and just how precious those child free moments are, so again, thank you for spending some of those moments with me. As a teacher, I want to thank you for your efforts in ensuring your child is school ready, it really does make our job easier. Strong, supportive partnerships between teachers and parents are so important. I hope you found this book to be useful in sparking a love of learning in your little one and preparing them for big school. May they walk through that classroom door with confidence.

To Kat Richardson, my illustrator, designer, editor, advisor and all-round book expert…wow… where do I even start. Thank goodness I found you. Thank you for bringing my very specific vision to life. You have held my hand through every step of the process. Thank you for answering the million and one questions I've asked. Your illustrations are absolutely stunning, and you have exceeded my expectations in every area. If anyone out there is after an amazing illustrator, designer or editor check out @katrich.creative on Instagram.

To Kade, my beautiful boy, thank you for being a champion sleeper and allowing me time to write this book. I promise to one day put my words into action and ensure you are a confident learner and begin Prep feeling school ready.

To Calvin, my husband. Thank you for always supporting me and for making me a mother.

To Mum, thank you for formatting my mess of a document so I could submit it for editing. Maybe one day I'll get the hang of page breaks and bullet points.

To Linny, my oldest and best friend. Thank you for always being my number one supporter in everything I do. How special it is to raise our children at the same time.

To all my teacher friends, thank you for always inspiring me and helping me to be better. I wouldn't be the teacher I am today without you.

Danielle x

Notes

www.ingramcontent.com/pod-product-compliance
Lightning Source LLC
Chambersburg PA
CBHW040741020526
44107CB00084B/2830